35MM PHOTOGRAPHY SIMPLIFIED

A MODERN PHOTOGUIDE

35MM PHOTOGRAPHY SIMPLIFIED

by

The Amphoto Editorial Board

PRENTICE-HALL
Englewood Cliffs, New Jersey 07632

AMPHOTO
Garden City, New York 11530

The following companies have cooperated
in the preparation of this book:

Typesetting:	Radnor Graphic Arts Radnor, Pennsylvania.
All paper:	Westvaco Luke, Maryland.
Printing:	Hallmark Lithographers, Inc. Westbury, New York.
Binding:	AME Bindery Jersey City, New Jersey.

Published in Garden City, New York by American Photographic Book Publishing Co., Inc.

Manufactured in the United States of America.
Library of Congress Catalog Number—73-92423
ISBN—0-8174-0197-0 (Softbound edition: Amphoto)
0-13-918870-3 (Softbound edition: Prentice-Hall)
0-13-918888-6 (Hardbound edition: Prentice-Hall)

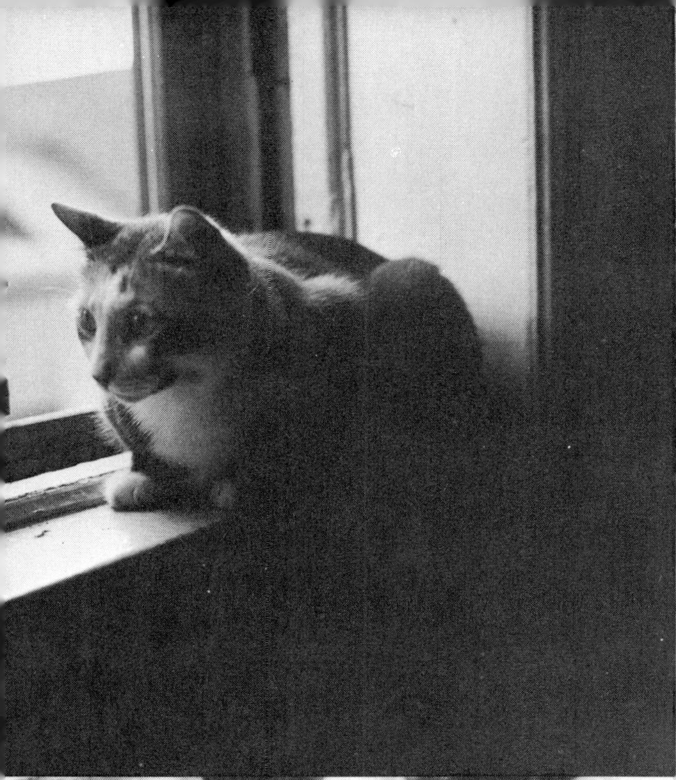
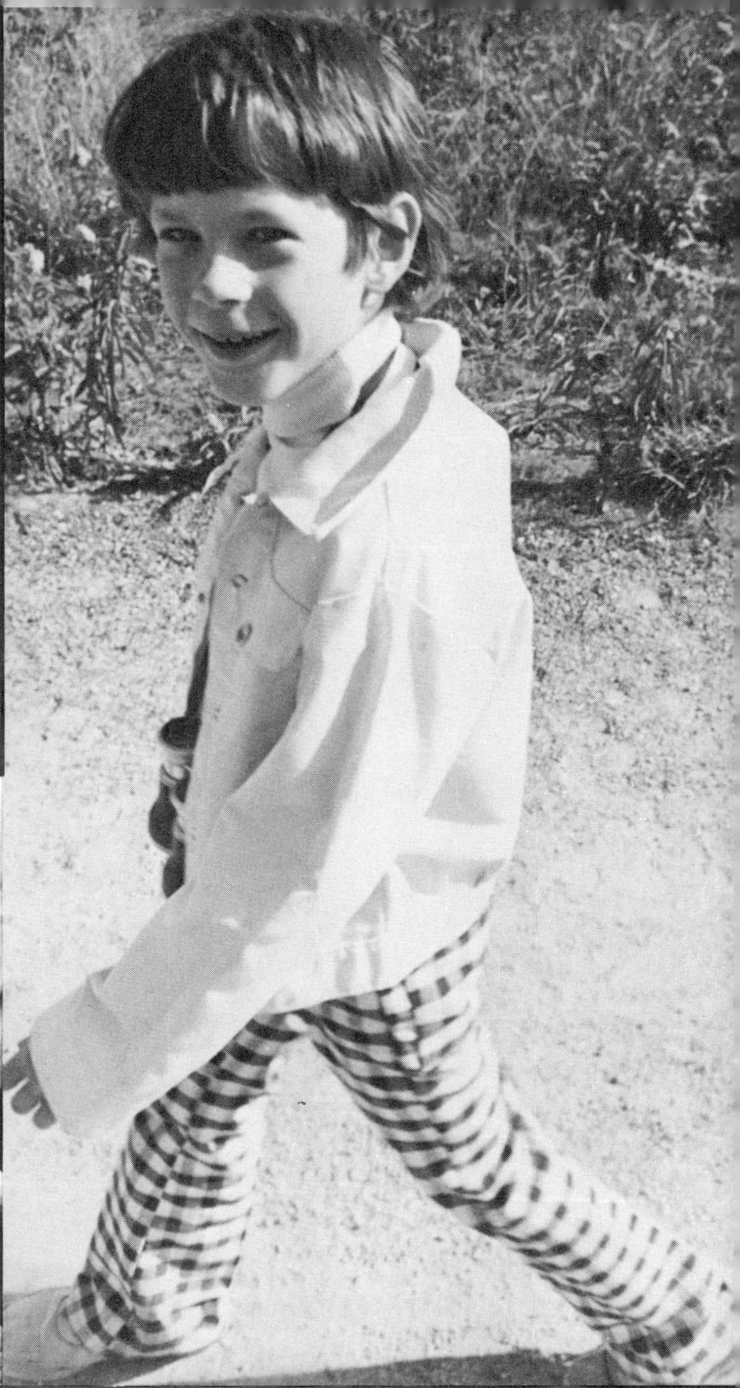
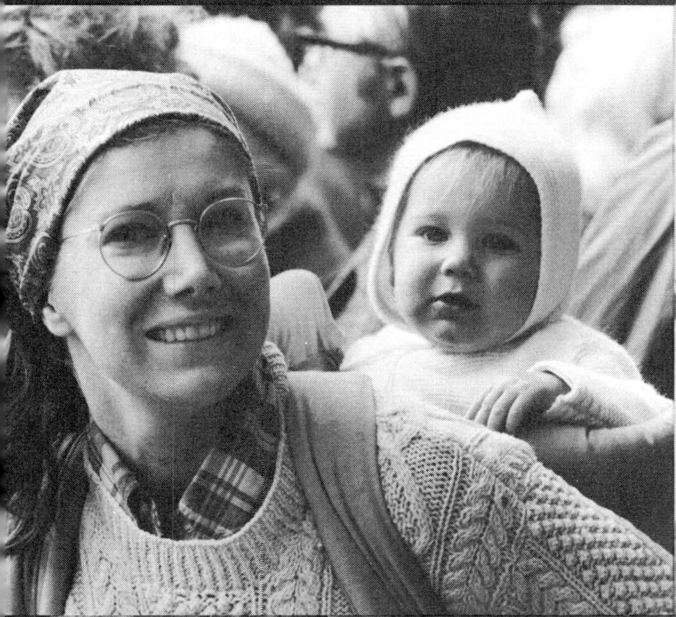
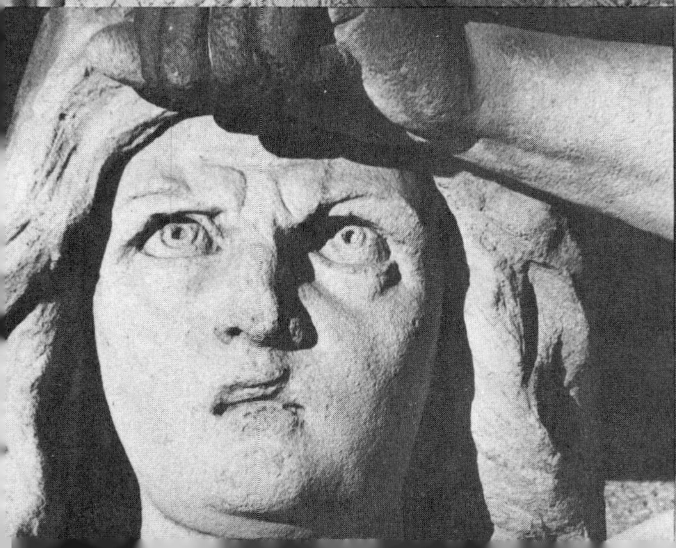
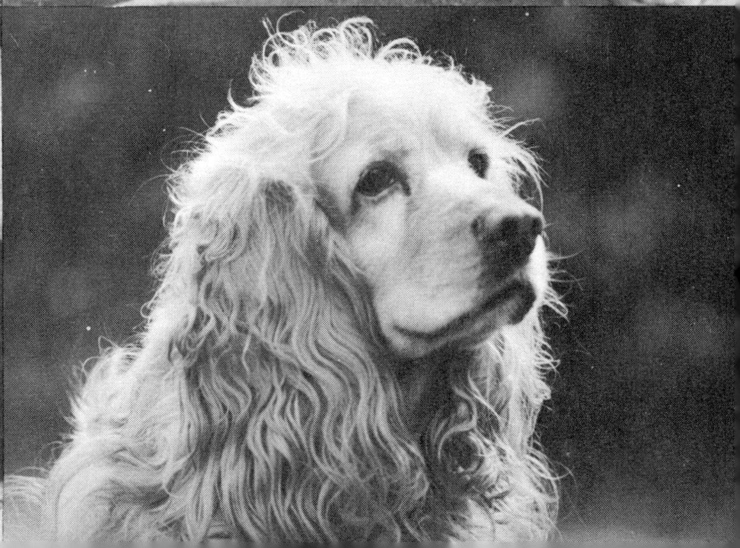

CONTENTS

INTRODUCTION

The 35mm camera is the most popular camera sold today, but many of the people who own these amazing miniatures do not utilize them to their fullest potential. The wonderful thing about 35mm photography is that there is always something new to learn, something new to try, something new to bring even more enjoyment to your picture taking.

This book will explain the fundamentals of photography—how your camera and film work and how you can best use them to achieve successful pictures. Beyond the how to, we will go on to explore the whats, and the whys, and the wheres of picture taking. For, these are the true how to's of photography—the elements that go into the making of a creative photograph.

Ideas of what to shoot, ways of extracting good pictures from seemingly mundane situations, the truly thought-out choice of lens, and the willingness to experiment will all expand the potential of your camera and the pleasure you take in your photographs.

In order to take good pictures, you must, logically, take pictures—and a good many of them. Professionals on assignment take roll upon roll of exposures to produce that one exposure that you see in your favorite newspaper or magazine. Remember that film is the least expensive aspect of photography. Don't shoot thoughtlessly—but never hesitate to shoot something that interests you for fear of wasting film. Film is much more easily replaced than a good shooting opportunity. Also, never limit your shooting of an interesting subject to one shot. Try different angles, different lenses, or even different exposures and see the variety one subject can present when you graduate from picturetaker to photographer.

We hope that you will find the technical portions of this book helpful and that the nontechnical sections will encourage experimentation. Good shooting.

The preparation of this book and other titles in The Modern Photoguide Series was supervised by Patricia Maye, Amphoto's Managing Editor. Ms. Maye also designed the book. Special thanks is due to Sheldon Czapnik, Judy Kiviat, and Penny J. Schwartz of the Amphoto Editorial staff for their cooperation in the preparation of the text material and to John C. Wolf, Amphoto's Editor-in-Chief for his helpful suggestions for improving the project overall. Thanks is also due to all the photographers who were kind enough to supply their material, especially to Rafael Fraguada who contributed so much of his time and so many of his photographs to the project.

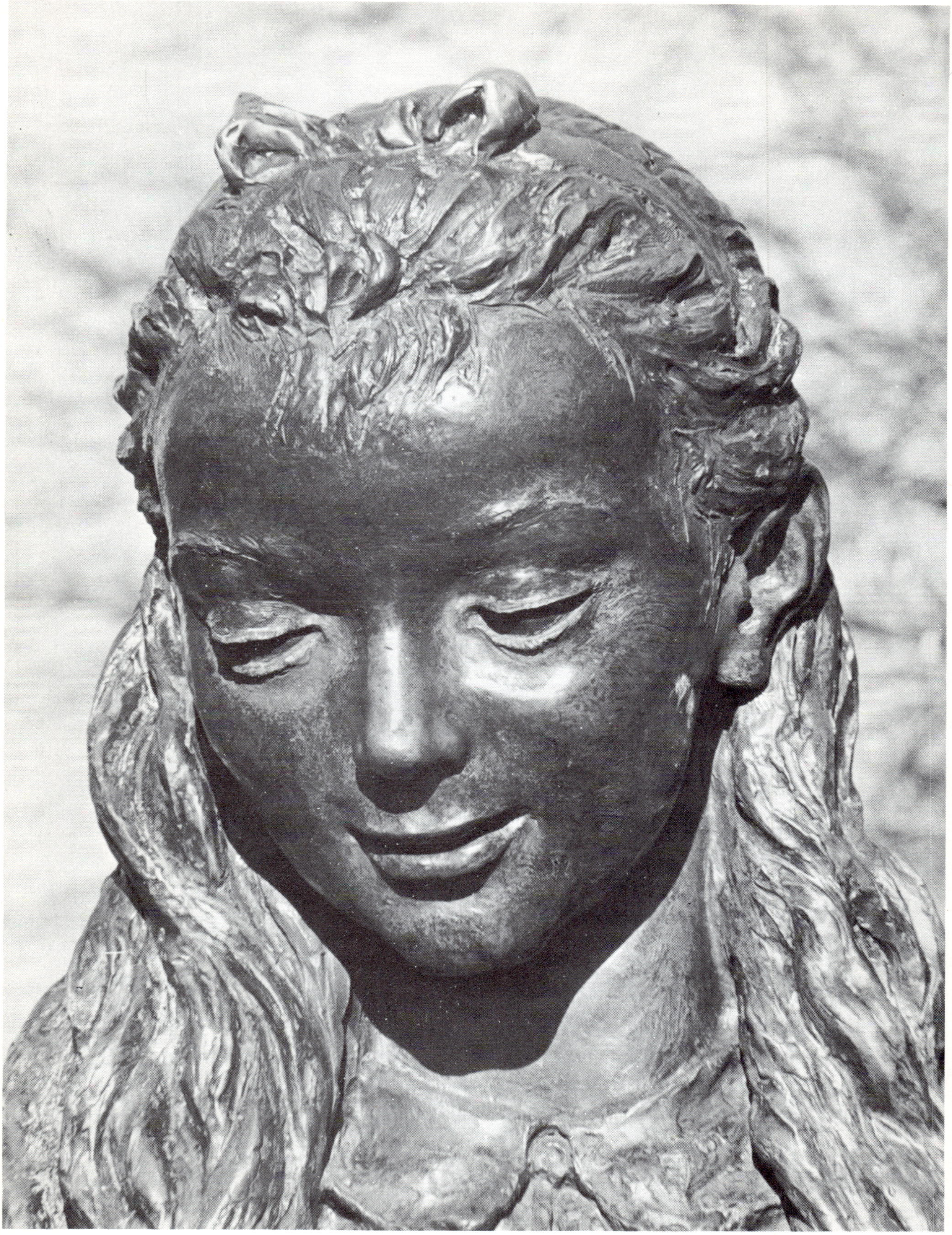

1

YOUR CAMERA AND LENS

The world of 35mm photography is an unqualified Wonderland. Hopefully, your exploration of it will prove as fascinating as Alice's trip through the looking glass. Photo by Rafael Fraguada.

YOUR CAMERA

The 35mm camera has become the workhorse for professional photographers the world over—and for very good reasons. It is compact, hardy and available in a range of makes, models, and prices to suit all purposes and pocketbooks.

The two main types of 35mm camera are the rangefinder and the single-lens reflex. The principal difference between the two is in the viewing system. The rangefinder views the subject through two separate windows at opposite sides of the top front of the camera. A double or split image appears in the viewer until the camera is correctly focused. Then, and only then, the images merge into a single clear image.

With the single-lens reflex, viewing is done directly through the lens. The image strikes a mirror within the camera body and is reflected up and through a prism at the top of the camera. Viewing is done through the back of the prism and as the lens is correctly focused the image becomes gradually sharp. When the picture is taken, the mirror flips up out of the way and the light passes through to the film.

Both types of camera have their fans. Rangefinder owners praise the quickness of focusing and the uncomplicated internal mechanics of their models. Single-lens reflex advocates stress the wider applicability of their cameras and the plus point that through-the-lens viewing allows for through-the-lens metering and exact pre-view of the picture about to be taken.

The strongest selling point of 35mm cameras is less interchangeability. The flexibility of being able to switch quickly from one lens to another expands the possibilities of your photography to the limits of your imagination (and, alas, of your budget). Through-the-lens viewing allows for use of lenses of any focal length on the SLR. Because the viewing system of the rangefinder is separate from the lens, frame-finder lines are inscribed within the viewer to show the edges of the image area with certain lenses. There is, of course, a practical limit to the number of lines able to be inscribed and understood. And, coupling a super-wide lens onto a rangefinder model would cause part of your picture area to fall outside the boundaries of the viewer, while with a super-long lens you'd be forced to focus on a small unmagnified section in the center of the view. Thus, the range of lenses able to be used with the rangefinder camera is more limited than with the SLR.

As indicated earlier, both types of camera have staunch supporters. Which would be best for you is up to you. Borrowing a camera from a trusting friend is the best way to try out a model before purchasing. Short of that, visit your camera store and handle the different models available until you find one that you feel comfortable with. Hands vary as much as do tastes and prejudices and even the best camera in the world might be wrong for you if it proves uncomfortable in your hand or awkward for you to use.

NORMAL LENS

Until recently the 50mm lens was thought of as the standard lens for a miniature camera. By many it still is. It is popular because of its versatility. A wide-angle effect can be created by stepping back and using the entire negative area, or cropping for a long, thin vertical or horizontal enlargement. You can also get a telephoto lens effect by cropping a section of the negative. The lens can be used for portraiture when you want a shot of your subject relating to his interests, rather than a straight head-and-shoulder portrait. This versatility, then, probably accounts for the fact that most pictures taken by amateurs today are made with the 50mm lens.

Professionals, however, now put the 35mm lens in the "normal" category. The primary reason for the switch is the 35mm's greater depth of field at normal picture-taking distances and its ability to take in a wider angle of view. Also, new versions of 35mm lenses are now being made in the large apertures formerly found only in the 50mm lens. If you must choose only two lens, you might well consider a 35mm and either an 85mm, 100mm or a 105mm, as being the two most versatile lenses in combination.

WIDE-ANGLE LENS

The wide-angle lens enables you to photograph a larger slice of a scene without stepping back, so it is ideal for shooting in confined or crowded places.

The normal 50mm lens has a 45-degree angle of view; a wide-angle lens of 25mm would have half its focal length, and take in twice as wide an arc—90 degrees. The most popular wide-angle lens is the 35mm, which covers 64 degrees and, which many contemporary photographers use as their standard lens.

Because of their short focal length, wide-angle lenses offer considerable depth of field and you can often get away with zone focusing, *i.e.*, preselecting a lens opening that gives a wide depth of field. (For example, with a 35mm lens set at *f*/8 and 15 feet on the footage scale, everything from 8′ to infinity will be in focus.)

One important point to remember when using a wide-angle lens is that it exaggerates or distorts objects which are close to you in the foreground—but this exaggeration can sometimes be effective if you use it for a purpose, for it can be used to create a feeling of power and drama. The wide-angle also distorts spherical objects at the extreme ends of the picture and the photographer must therefore be careful not to include this shape object or he will end up with oval-shaped heads, or something equally unusual.

The normal lens is useful for a variety of subjects—from close-range portraits through middle-range landscape studies to distant scenics. The slice of nature opposite was photographed at the New York Botanical Society Gardens in the Bronx with a 58mm normal lens. The natural perspective and good size rendition are characteristics of the normal lens. Photo by Rafael Fraguada.

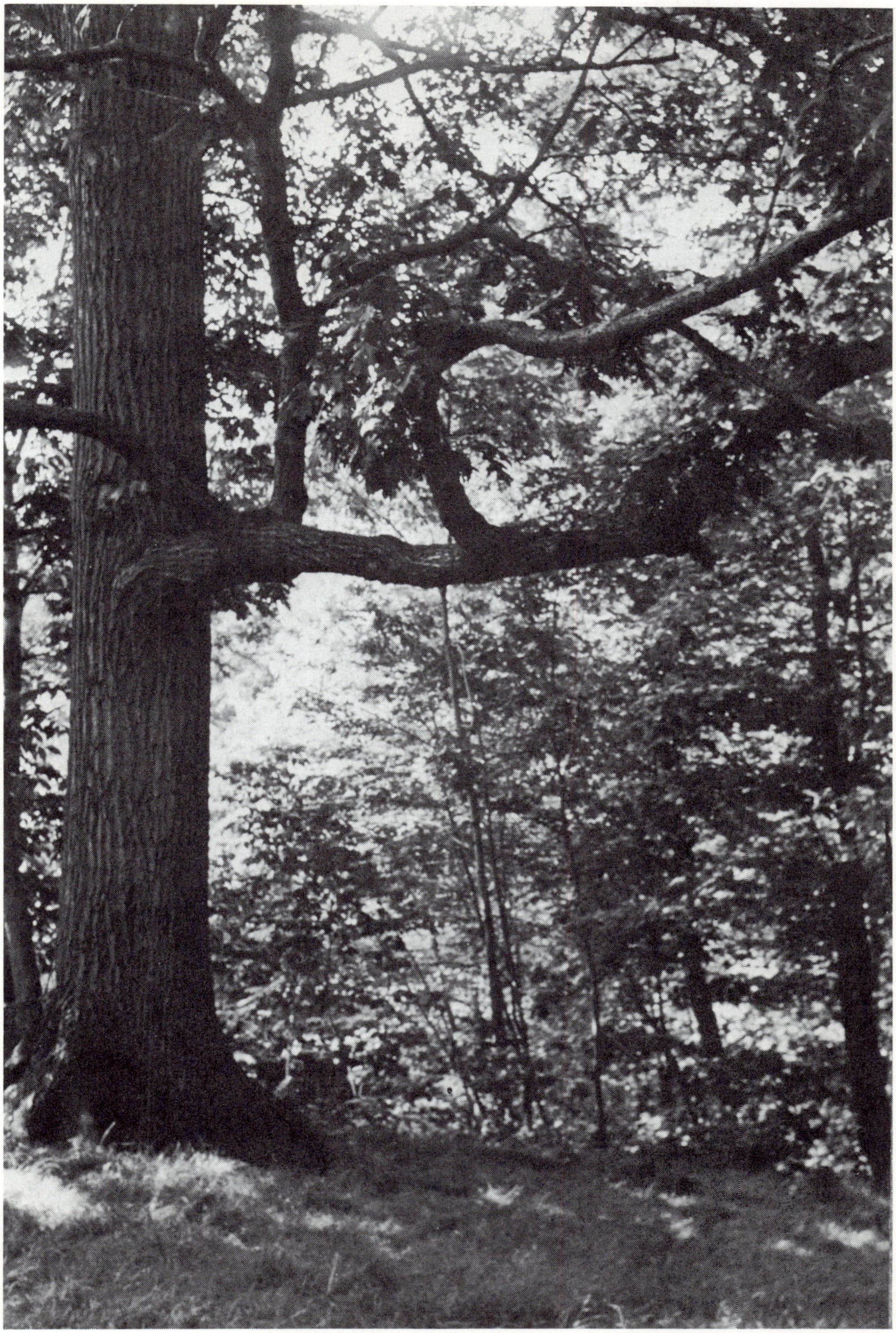

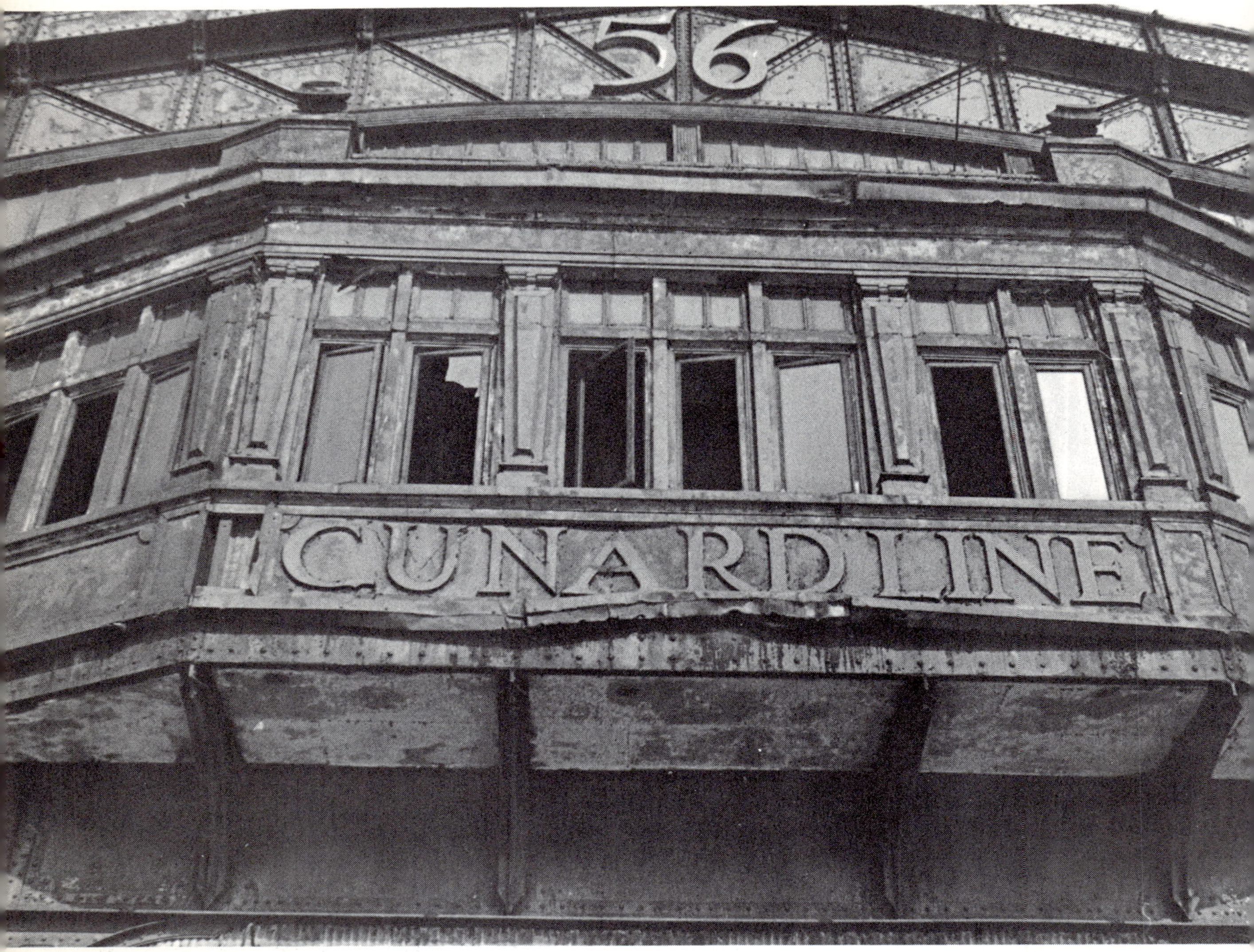

The wide-angle lens offers two important working assets to the photographer. Its generous angle of view allows for taking in a good deal of the subject at reasonably close quarters. This was a working necessity for the shot above—the photographer could not step any further back without stepping off the end of the pier.

A second attribute of the wide-angle lens is a deep in-focus area or "depth of field." In the photo opposite focus is sharp from the near gangplank through the doorway with the eerie figure in the background. Both photos were taken with a 35mm Miranda lens. Photos by Rafael Fraguada.

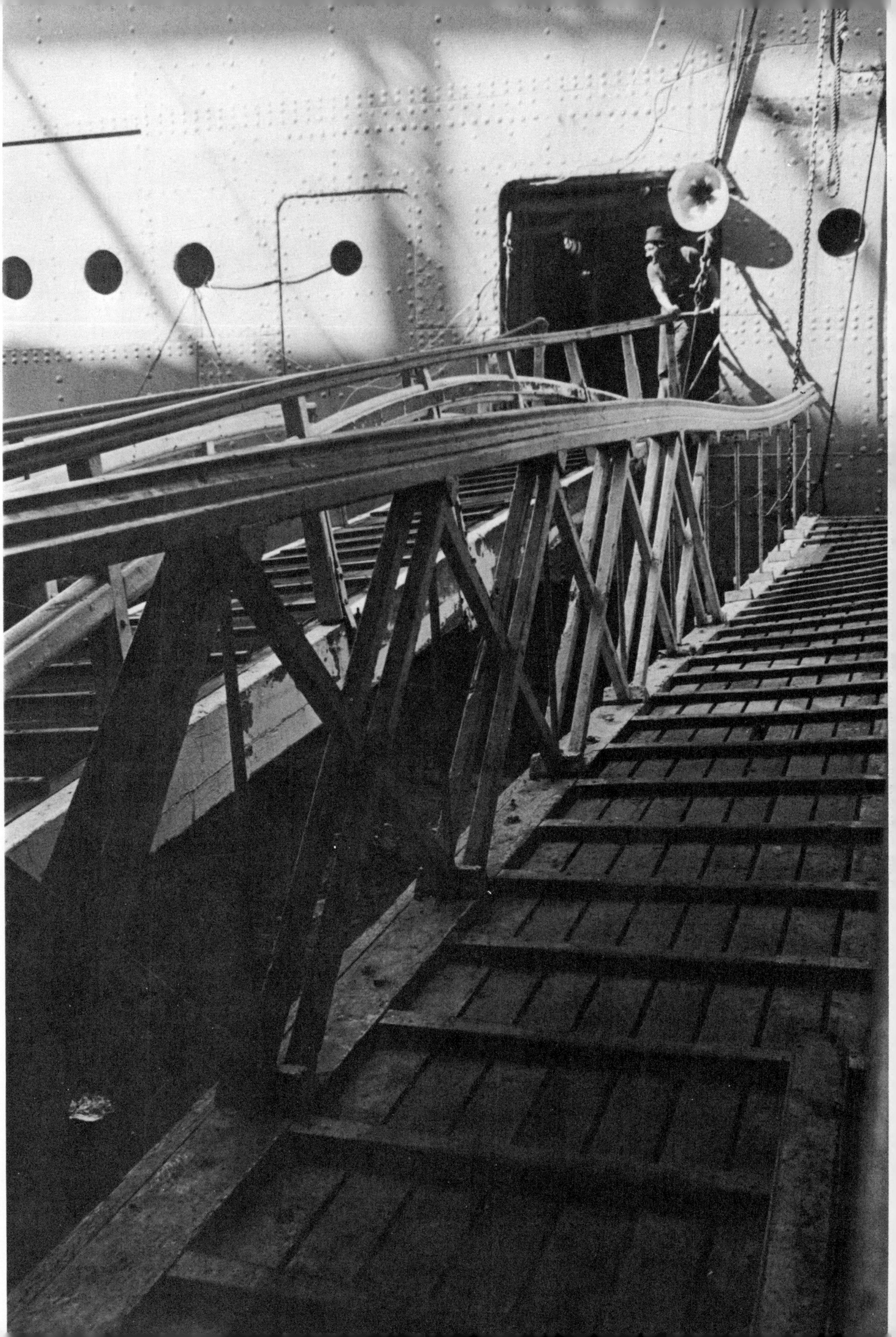

MEDIUM TELEPHOTO

The medium telephoto range includes any lens with a focal length of 85mm to 135mm. Compared to the normal 50mm lens, these lenses narrow the field of view, producing an image approximately twice as large, and can be used to pick out distant subject matter. The medium telephoto with its shorter depth of field helps you eliminate extraneous surroundings and emphasize your subject.

These lenses are popular for photographing in situations where you want spontaneity. By your standing farther away from the action, your subjects will be less conscious of the camera. This makes the lens especially good for overcoming stiffness in portraits and candids of people.

Medium telephotos eliminate the problem of distortion in portraiture—cauliflower ears in side views and elongated noses in front views both of which may occur when you step in too close with the 50mm lens to get a larger image.

LONG TELEPHOTO

Long telephoto lenses—150mm to 600mm —are used to magnify and bring distant objects "closer" to the camera. They also compress a scene that would appear too spread out and disorganized when shot with a normal lens. The long telephoto's ability to isolate creates strong design pictures. It gives the viewer a feeling of intimacy, of being close to what is going on. In addition, it can take you into inaccessible places. At a football game, shots taken from the sidelines with a 300mm lens give the feeling that the photographer was in the middle of the action.

As the focal length of your lenses gets longer you will need to increase film and shutter speeds and add a tripod to your equipment pack.

The distance between the Christmas-light display on New York's Lord & Taylor department store and the sparkling lights of the offices in the Empire State Building in the background is actually 5 city blocks. Photographed from a distance through a 135mm lens, the distance seems much shorter. Photo by Horst Schafer.

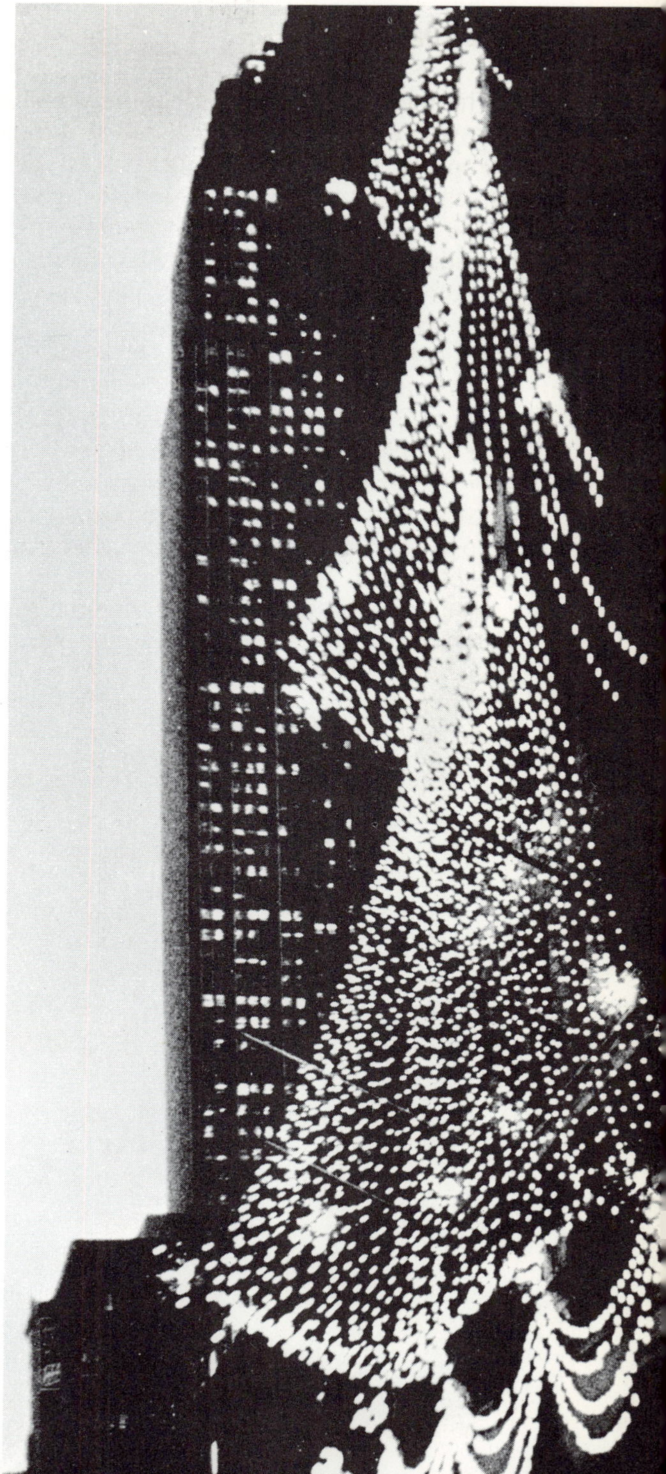

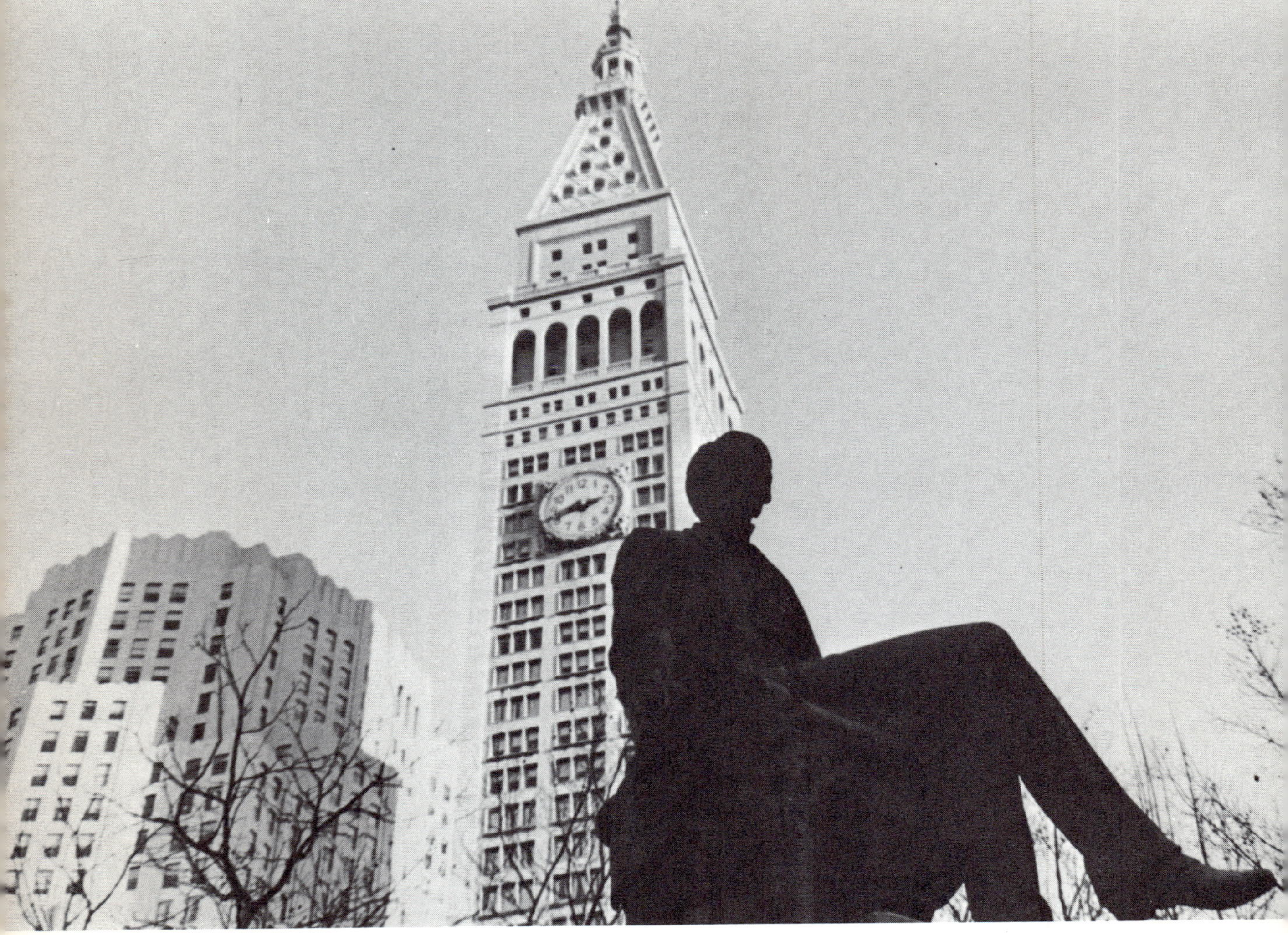

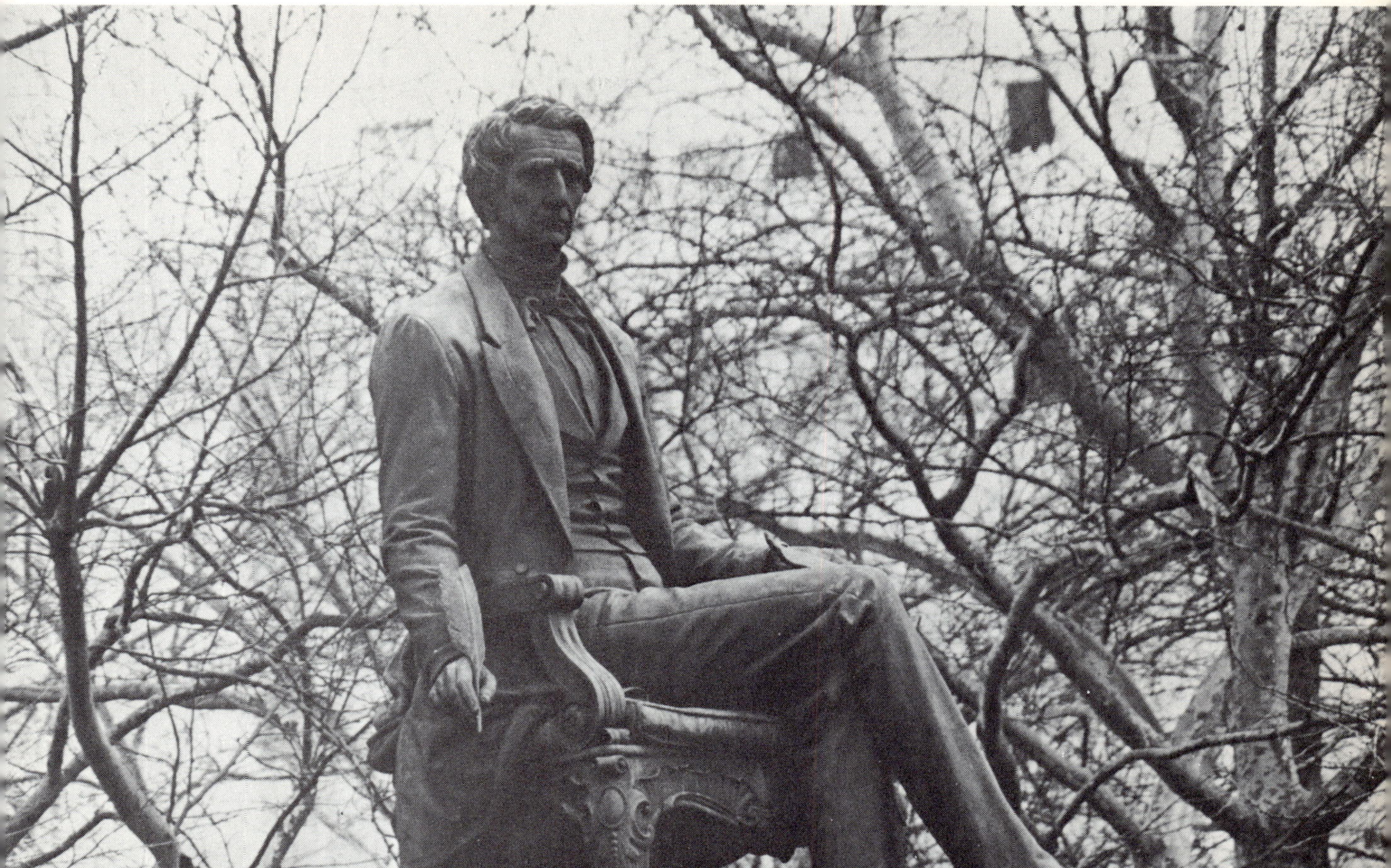

Shooting from a close distance with a wide-angle lens, the photographer was able to take in the entire sculpted figure in the photo opposite. Because of the shooting angle, the figure is seen in an unnatural perspective. The foot is rendered very large, the head, quite small. For the photo above, the photographer moved away to a good distance from the statue. Shooting with a Soligor 75-260 zoom lens set at its longest focal length, he achieved a good image size and a more normal perspective. Photos by Rafael Fraguada.

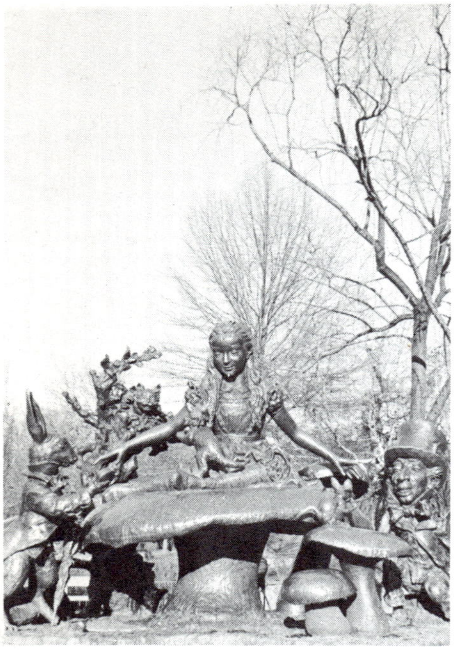

The wide-angle lens was used to photograph the entire sculpture group from about fifteen feet away. When the same lens was used for the detail of Alice's face, the features were rendered as overly prominent bulges. Photographed from further away with a zoom lens set at about 125mm, Alice appears as her pretty self. Making the Mad Hatter (opposite) handsome lay beyond the capabilities of any lens. Photos by Rafael Fraguada.

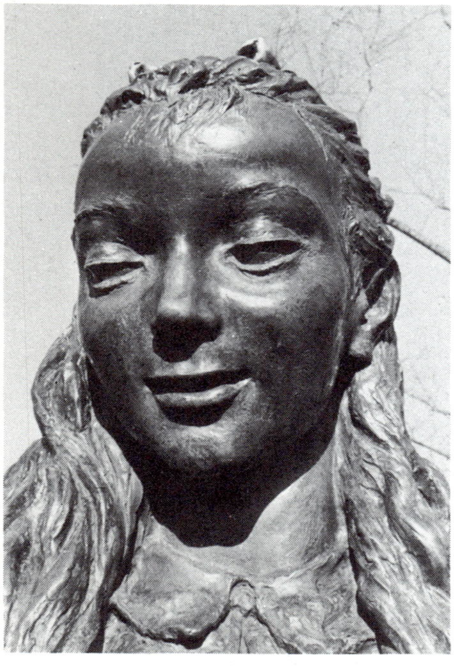

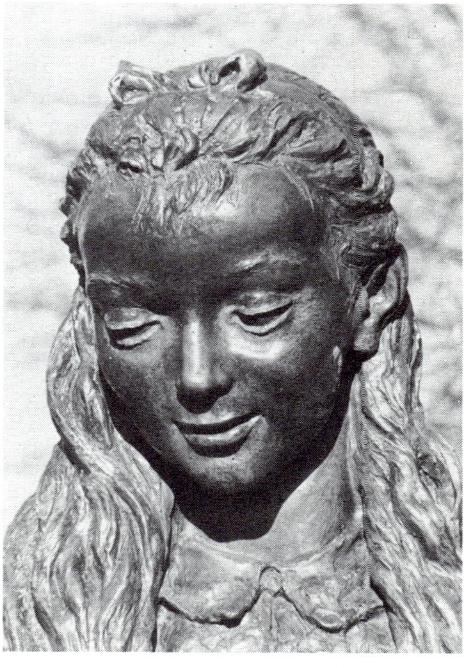

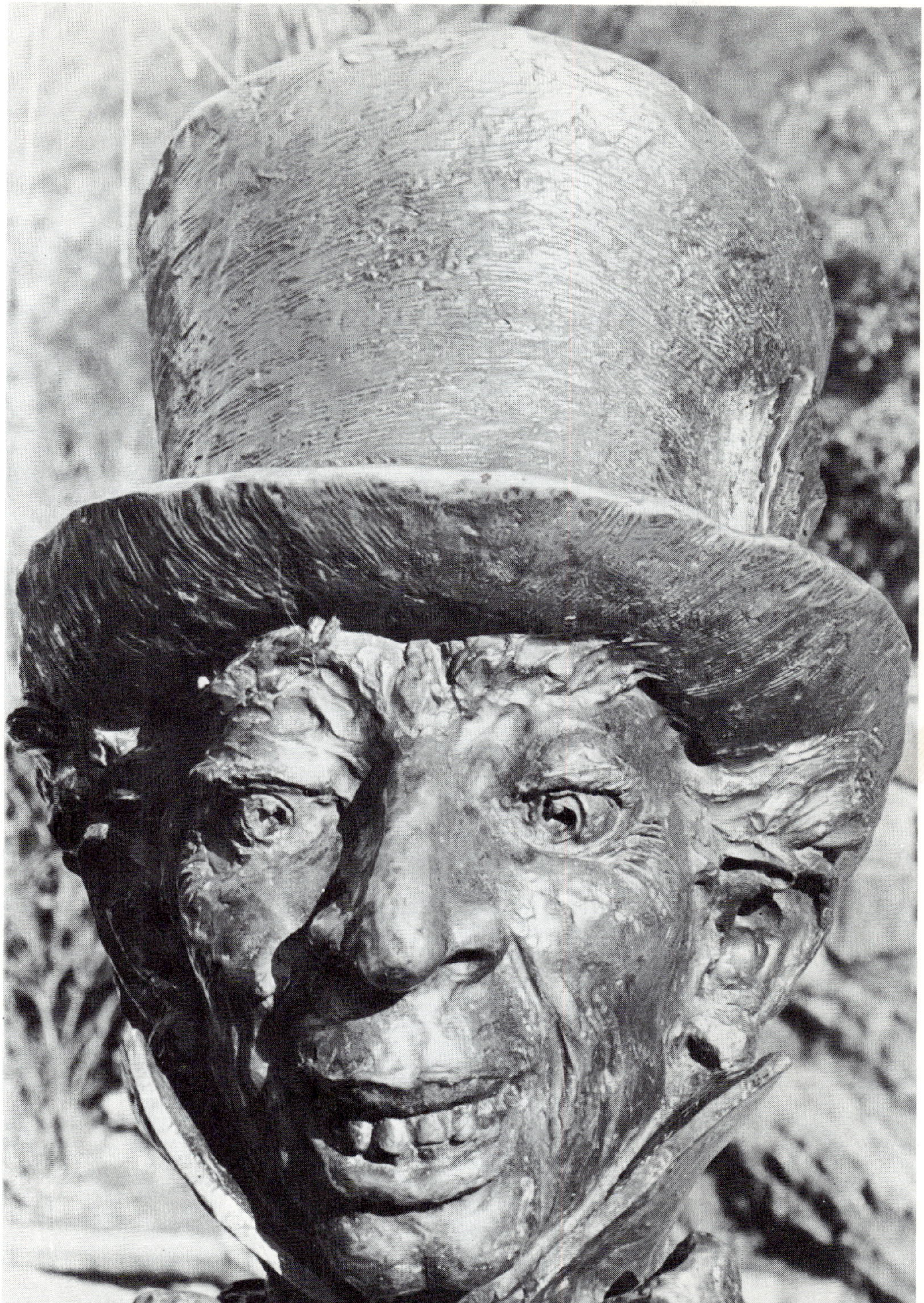

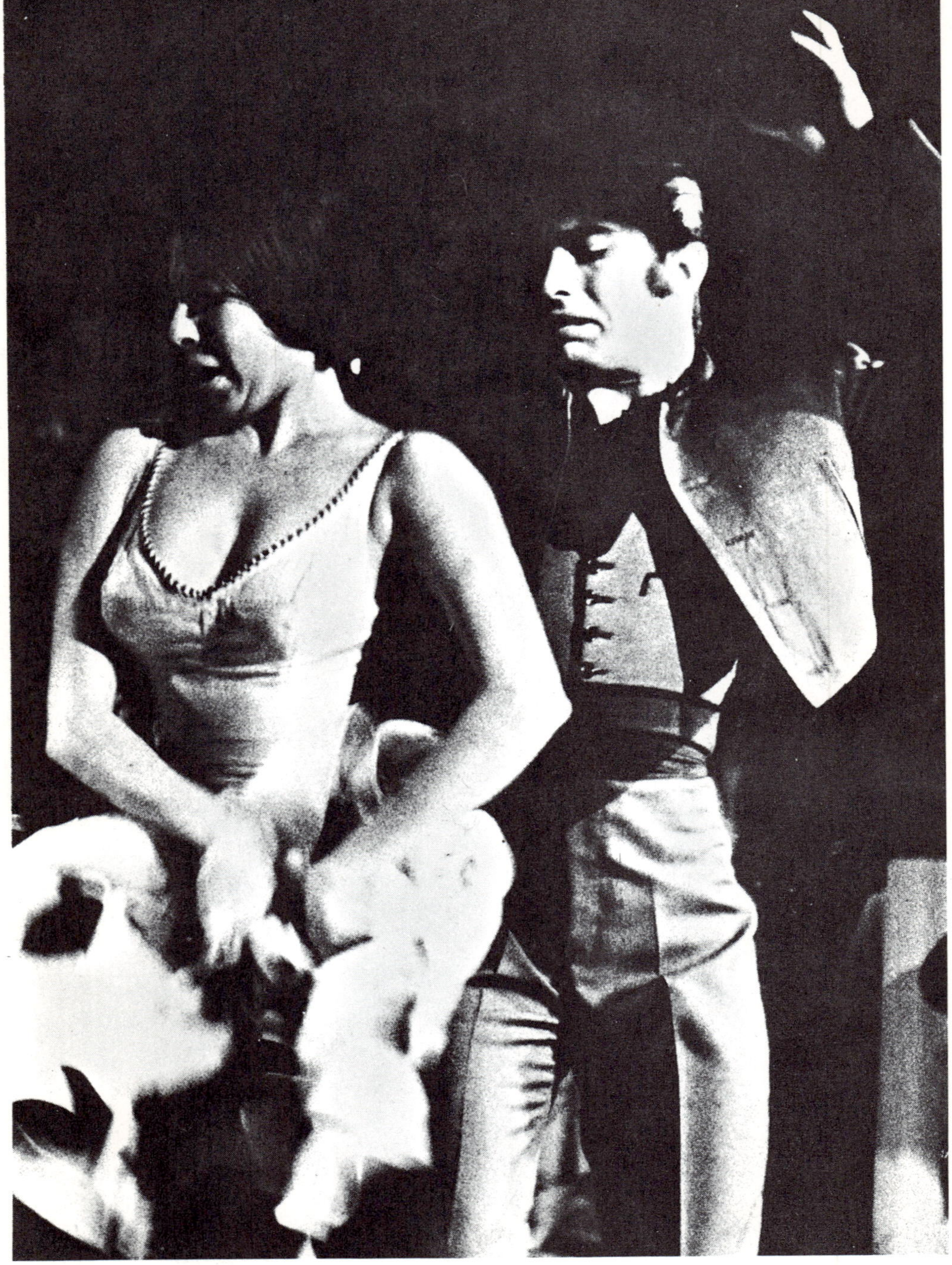

2

FILMS FOR BLACK-AND-WHITE AND COLOR PHOTOGRAPHY

High-speed films and special processing techniques have put low-light photography within the realm of possibility to the 35mm photographer. The photo of the flamenco dancers opposite was taken on Tri-X film rated at ASA 1200 and push-processed in Acufine. Photo by Kathy Wersen.

FILMS

A great variety of films, both black-and-white and color, are available to the 35mm camera owner. So many, in fact, that choosing one may be an altogether confounding experience to the novice. Your choice must be related to a number of factors—the types of pictures you intend to take, the light conditions under which they will be taken, and the final use to which you hope to put them. Shooting high-speed action or under poor light conditions would call for a super-light-sensitive film. A fine-detail, grainless, studio-type portrait would require a fine-grain black-and-white film. And, if color slides for lecture or show were your intended end results, you'd need a color slide (reversal) film. Light sensitivity, graininess, and the different kinds of color films are discussed in the following text in the hope of clarifying somewhat the matter of film choice.

Light sensitivity: All films bear a numerical rating, commonly called ASA, of their light sensitivity. A film with a low ASA number is less light sensitive than one with a higher number. A doubling of the ASA rating represents a doubling of sensitivity and a reduction to one half of the exposure necessary to produce an image. Thus, to produce a correct exposure, a film rated at ASA 200 would require only half as much light as would a film rated at ASA 100. ASA ratings are based on normal subjects, normal exposures, and normal processing procedures. The stated ASA ratings of films can be doubled or even tripled by special overprocessing. Such "push-processing" should, however, remain an emergency measure and not become standard operating procedure.

High speed black-and-white films with base ratings around ASA 1000 are now widely available in 35mm size. They can be push-processed to ratings of ASA 2000 and higher. They are a godsend for low-light shooting, but they yield images of diminished quality.

Tri-X film, base rated at ASA 400, has become the standard working film for many professionals—it is especially favored by working photojournalists who are continually confronted by a variety of available-light conditions. It is good for general shooting and can, when necessary, be pushed to ASA 1200 without a too apparent loss of image quality.

Grain: The light-sensitive emulsion on your film is a sophisticated chemical mix containing small particles of silver. In low ASA films the concentration of the silver particles tends to be thin and the particles small—thus, the need for greater amount of light to produce an image and the resulting fineness of that image. Fast films have an emulsion with more densely concentrated, larger grains and are thus bound to yield an image with less exposure but one characterized by apparent grain in enlargement. And, push-processing further emphasizes grain.

Color films: Unlike black-and-white films, which yield negatives, color films come in two popular types—one to produce negatives from which color prints can be made, the other to produce transparencies. Choose according to the end result you have in mind. Slides can be made into prints, but an intermediary color negative must be made first at additional cost and loss of image quality. Kodacolor, Ektacolor, Fugicolor and Agfacolor are all popular films for prints. Kodachrome, Ektachrome, Fugichrome, and Agfachrome are color slide films.

Color films are generally ASA rated lower than black-and-white films. For low-light and night shooting Kodak offers High Speed Ektachrome rated at ASA 160 while GAF has GAF 200 and GAF 500 Color Slide Films. The ratings of both these films can be doubled through special push-processing ordered at extra cost. Like fast black-and-white films, fast color films tend to be grainy. They also produce high contrast images with the shadow areas going black and without detail. They have, however, opened up available-light color shooting to the 35mm photographer.

Popular black-and-white and color films, their ratings, and applications are listed in the accompanying chart for your convenience.

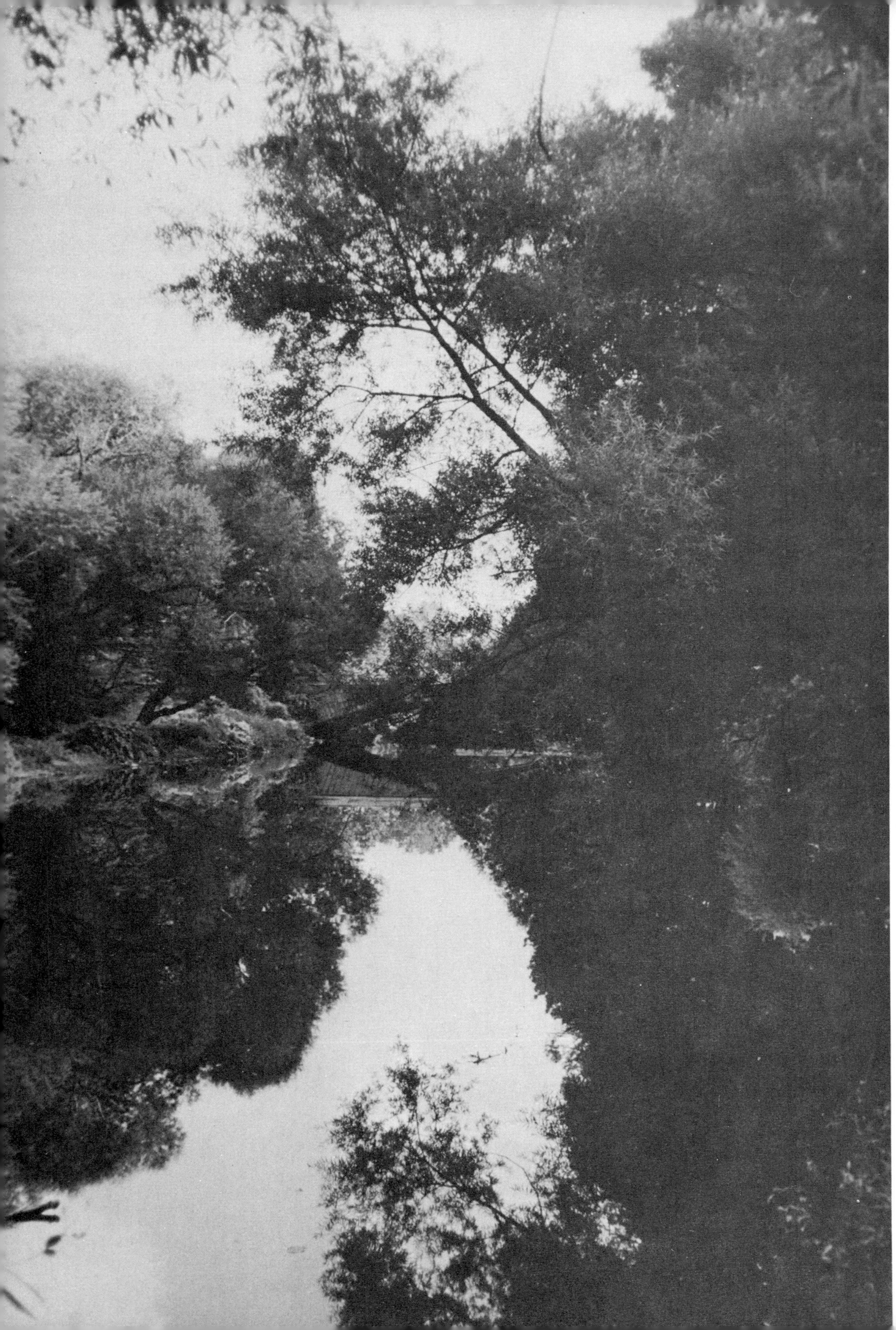

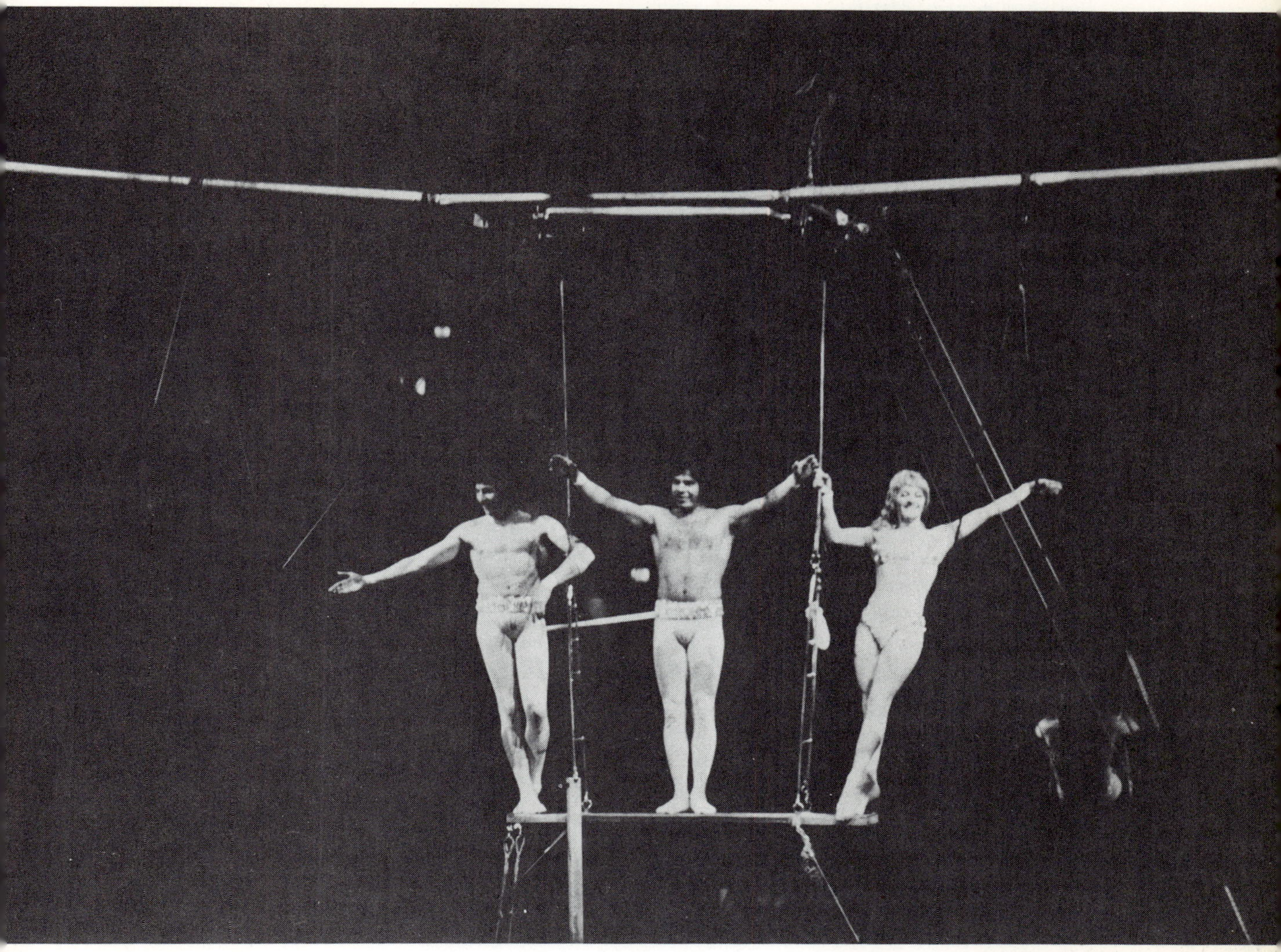

Modern films exist in such bewildering profusion that many photographers remain confused as to which to buy for certain subjects and light conditions. Happily some films have a wide enough exposure latitude to accommodate many shooting needs. Both the photos on these pages were taken on Tri-X film. Exposure and processing for the shot at left were normal. For the shot above, the film was rated at ASA 1000 and push processed by a custom lab. Photos by Rafael Fraguada.

FILMS AND DEVELOPERS

Photography is much more than taking a picture, and once you've stopped sending your film to the drug store or local photo processor you will find that a whole new area of fun and creativity has been opened up to you.

If you've had little or no darkroom experience you'd do well to standardize on one or a maximum of two films. For example, Tri-X for low light situations, Plus-X or Panatomic-X for daylight shots. Once you feel you can handle one or two films and one or two developers well, it will be time enough to try your wings on the many other fine products on the market. Many beginners experiment with many films and developers—and never learn the full potentials of any combination. Instead of using a variety of films for a variety of situations, you can rate Plus-X at two speeds and Tri-X at three (see the following charts). This solves the problem of carrying many different kinds of films and you'll never need to worry about running short. In bright sunlight when Plus-X at 200 is too fast you can use a filter (K2) to cut the speed back one stop—changing the ASA rating to 100. The accompanying chart lists suggested film, exposure rating, and development combinations that allow for rating only three films for exposure in situations from very bright through quite dim.

To adjust this information to your working needs, choose your film and developers, then process a few rolls of film according to these charts. If the negatives come out underexposed, check your method of meter reading. If there is no fault here, increase the development times; decrease development time for overexposed negatives, until you arrive at a relatively printable negative. Standardize on your new developing time. Consistently good negatives come from standardized developing procedures and meter readings.

PANATOMIC-X

ASA 40	D76 1:1*	70°	7 min.
ASA 100	Acufine	70°	3-4 min.

PLUS-X

ASA 200	D76 1:1	70°	8 min.
ASA 400	D76 1:1	70°	10-11 min.
ASA 400	Acufine	70°	5-5 1/5 min.

Plus-X at 400 is usually better in Acufine, but if you only have D76 it can be used adequately.

TRI-X

ASA 400	D76 straight**	70°	8 min.
ASA 800	D76 straight	70°	10-11 min.
ASA 800	Acufine	70°	4 1/2 min.
ASA 1200	Acufine	70°	5-5 1/2 min.

* 1:1 means one part developer to one part water. Throw it away after one time use.
** D76 straight means use stock developer as per instructions on can.

When pushing badly underexposed film in Acufine you can develop up to 12 minutes—after this nothing will happen.

POPULAR 35mm BLACK-AND-WHITE FILMS

Low-Speed, Fine-Grain Films
ASA 25-64

Ilford Pan-F	ASA 50
Kodak Panatomic X	32
H & W Control VTE Pan	80
H & W Control VTE Ultra	32

Medium-Speed, Moderate-Grain Films
ASA 125-400

Ilford FP4	ASA 125
Kodak Plus-X	125
Fuji Neopan SSS	200
Ilford HP4	400
Kodak Tri-X	400

High-Speed, Coarser-Grain Films
ASA over 400

Kodak Tri-X	Overrated and push-processed at ratings from 800-1200 ASA
Kodak 2475 Recording Film	ASA 1000

Applications

Low-speed, fine-grain films are especially useful in shooting well-lit, static subjects such as landscapes or for portraits taken in full sunlight. The low ASA rating is a shortcoming when these films are considered for all-around work, but the almost grainless negatives they produce through correct exposure and processing yield handsome enlargements full of detail and free of discernible grain even in large size prints.

Medium-speed, moderate-grain films are among the most popular films on the market today. They can be used in a variety of lighting situations and for almost any subject. In enlargement, grain does not become a factor if the films have been exposed and developed according to manufacturers' specifications.

High-speed, coarser-grain films are designed for shooting in low-light situations. Tri-X appears twice in the chart above because many photographers, when shooting in low light or at night, use Tri-X and deliberately overrate it at high ASA ratings. The overdeveloping that such personal ASA adjustments necessitates increases the probability of visible grain in enlargement. ASA adjustments should be reserved for shooting situations where nothing else will do the trick. Truly high-speed films such as the 2475 Recording film listed above have low contrast and should be used only when the high speed is absolutely necessary. Night or low-light shots usually have built-in contrast. If the film is used in well-lit surroundings the resulting photos will lack zip.

POPULAR 35MM COLOR FILMS

For Color Slides

	ASA (daylight)	ASA (tungsten-3200K)
Agfachrome CT 18 (D)	50	12 (a)
3M Brand Color Slide (D)	50	16 (a)
Ektachrome-X (D)	64	16 (a)
High-Speed Ektachrome (D)	160	40 (a)
High-Speed Ektachrome (T)	80 (b)	125
Fujichrome R-100 (D)	100	25 (a)
GAF 64 Color Slide Film (D)	64	16 (a)
GAF 200 Color Slide Film (D)	200	80 (a)
GAF t/100 Color Slide Film (T)	64 (b)	100
GAF 500 Color Slide Film (D)	500	125 (a)
Kodachrome II (D)	25	6 (a)
Kodachrome-X (D)	64	16 (a)

For Negatives and Prints

Agfacolor CNS (D)	80	20 (a)
Ektacolor Professional Type S (D)	100	25 (a)
Kodacolor-X (D)	80	20 (a)
Sakuracolor Color Print Film (D)	80	20 (a)

(D) color balanced for daylight, blue-flash, or electronic-flash exposure
(T) color balanced for exposure by tungsten illumination
(a) exposed through an 80A filter
(b) exposed through an 85B filter

Applications

Color-film emulsions are much more sophisticated than those used for black-and-white films. Color films are "color-balanced" for use with specific light sources. The "D" or "T" inserted after each film name in the list above indicates whether that film is balanced for exposure by daylight or tungsten illumination. Daylight films can be used for natural light shooting *plus* exposures made with a daylight-matched, electronic-flash unit or blue flashbulbs or cubes. Tungsten films are balanced for use with incandescent illumination such as photographers' studio lamps or clear flashbulbs. They will give the most naturalistic color rendition when photos are taken by household, bulb-type lamps.

The coding "(a)" and "(b)" in the listing above refers to the type or filter to be used if daylight film is to be exposed by tungsten illumination or if tungsten film is to be exposed by daylight, electronic flash, or blue flashbulbs.

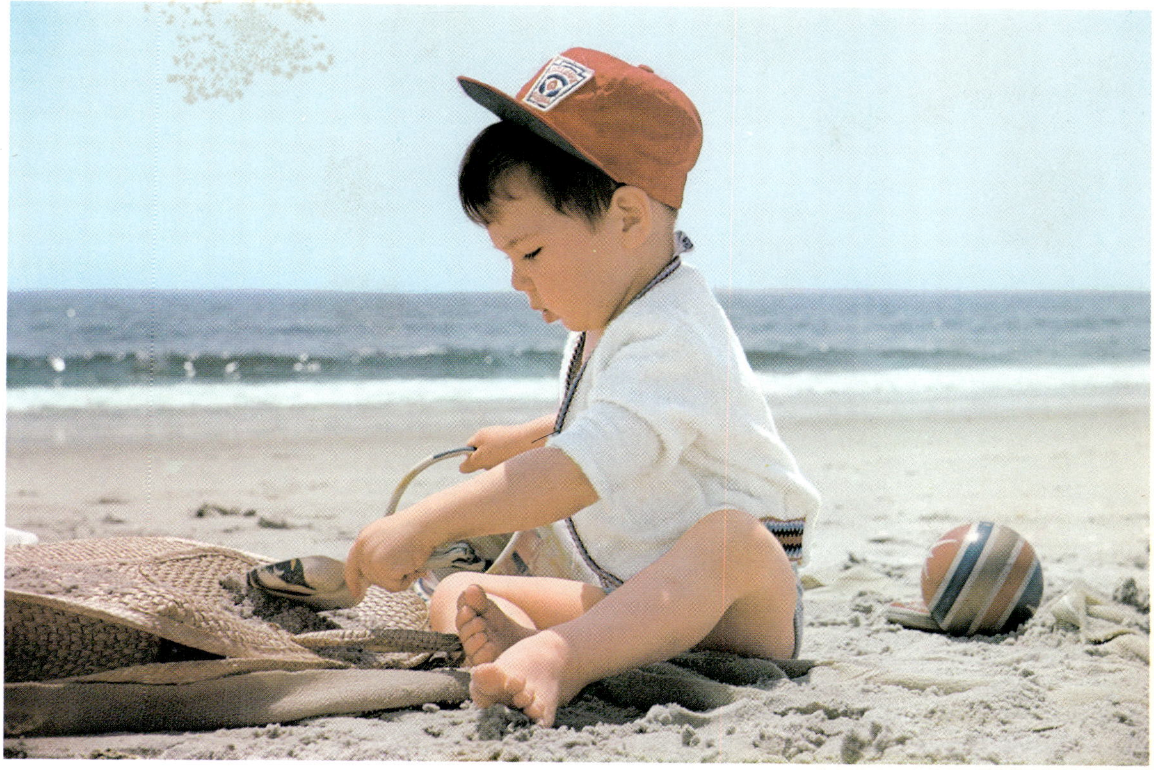

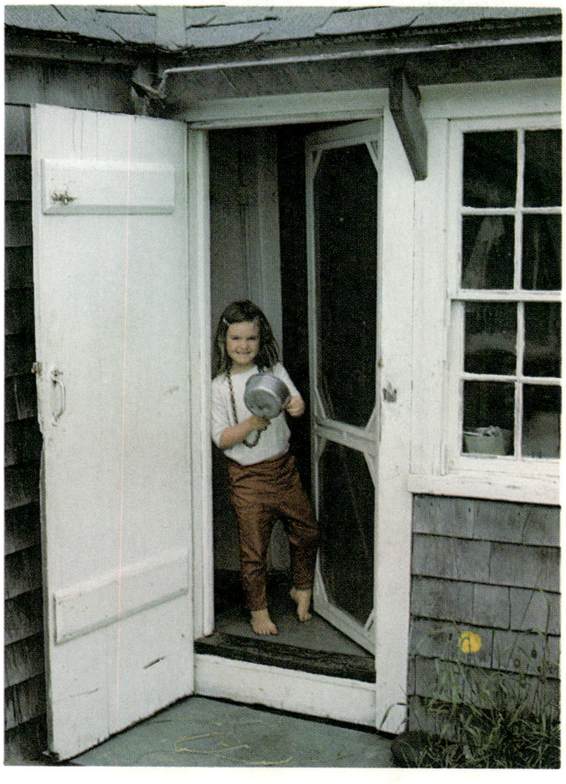

Children are a favorite subject for color photography. Usually the subject is interesting enough in itself to make any photographic frills or flourishes unnecessary. Indeed—more often than not—so-called "special effects" prove inappropriate to the photography of children. Both the photos on this page were shot with a normal lens with the subjects unposed. The young boy above was photographed in the early morning when the sun was bright but not blistering. The shadows were softened by the sunlight being bounced up from the sand. Cropping was kept tight to concentrate attention on the boy's involvement in his task of burying the photographer's handbag. A reprimand would have saved the bag but ruined the shot. The portrait of the little girl at right was photographed from a greater distance to include the framing doorway and weathered wood of the house—her summer home. An overcast day provided shadowless light and lent a pleasant overall blue cast to the picture. Photos by Patricia Maye.

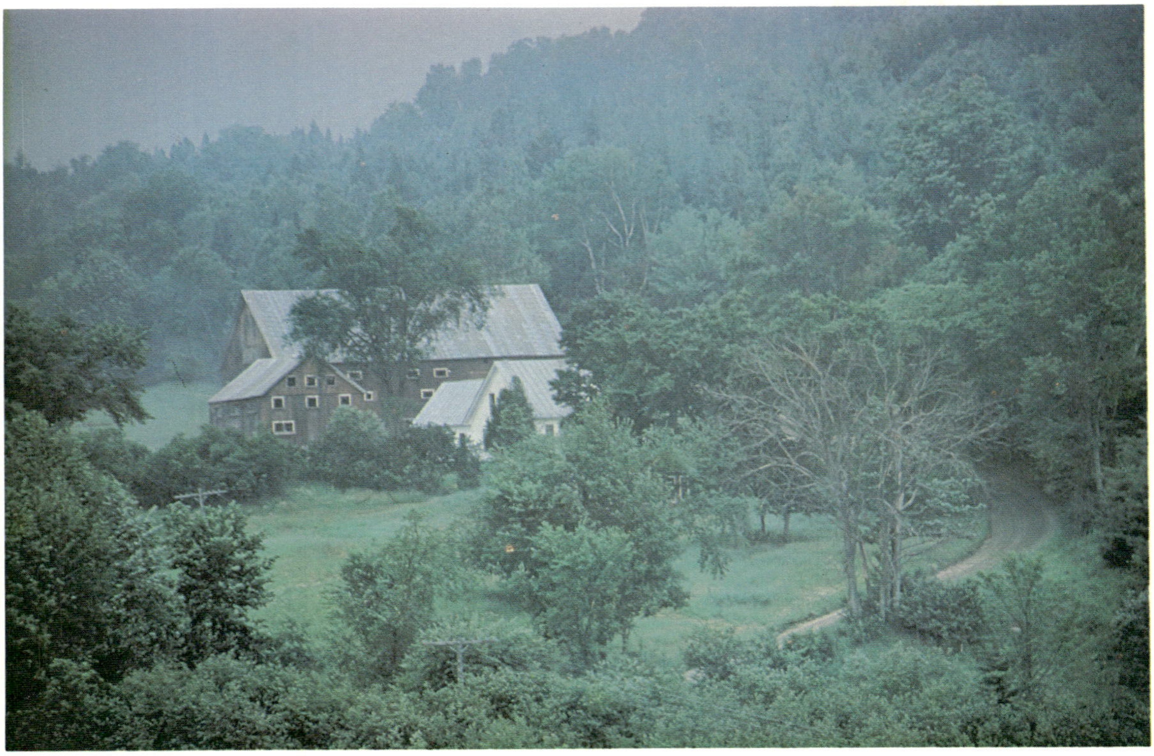

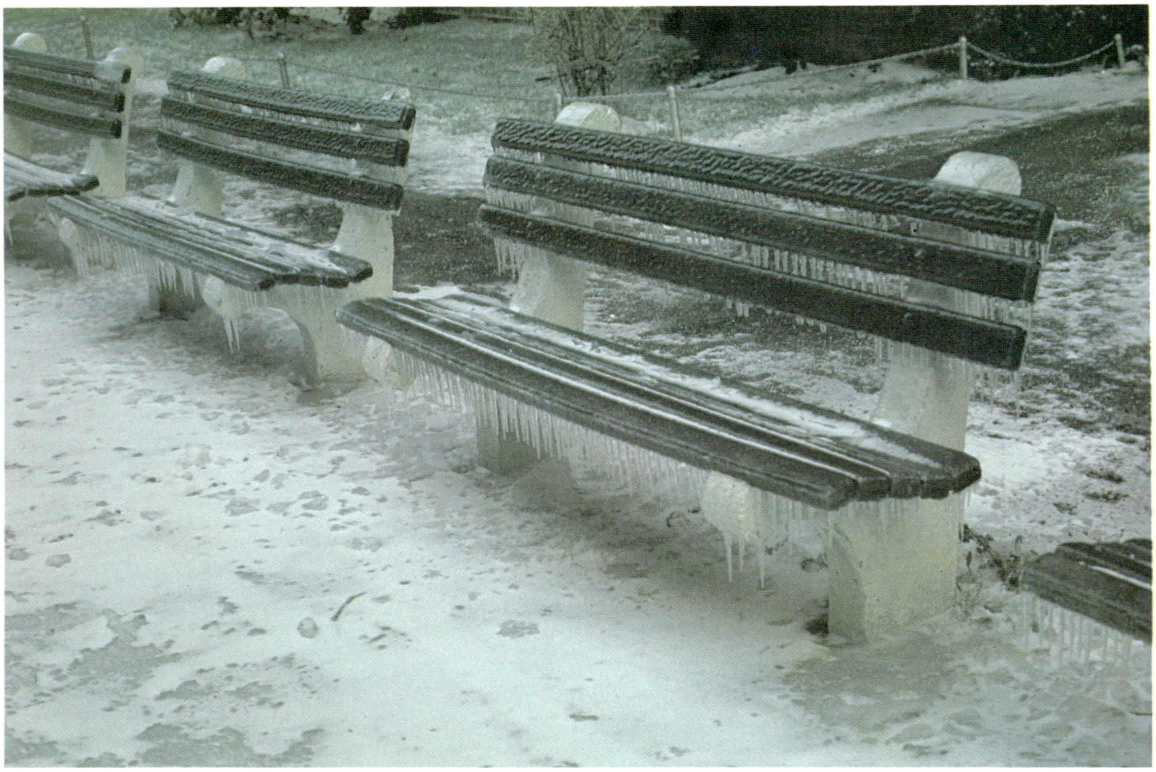

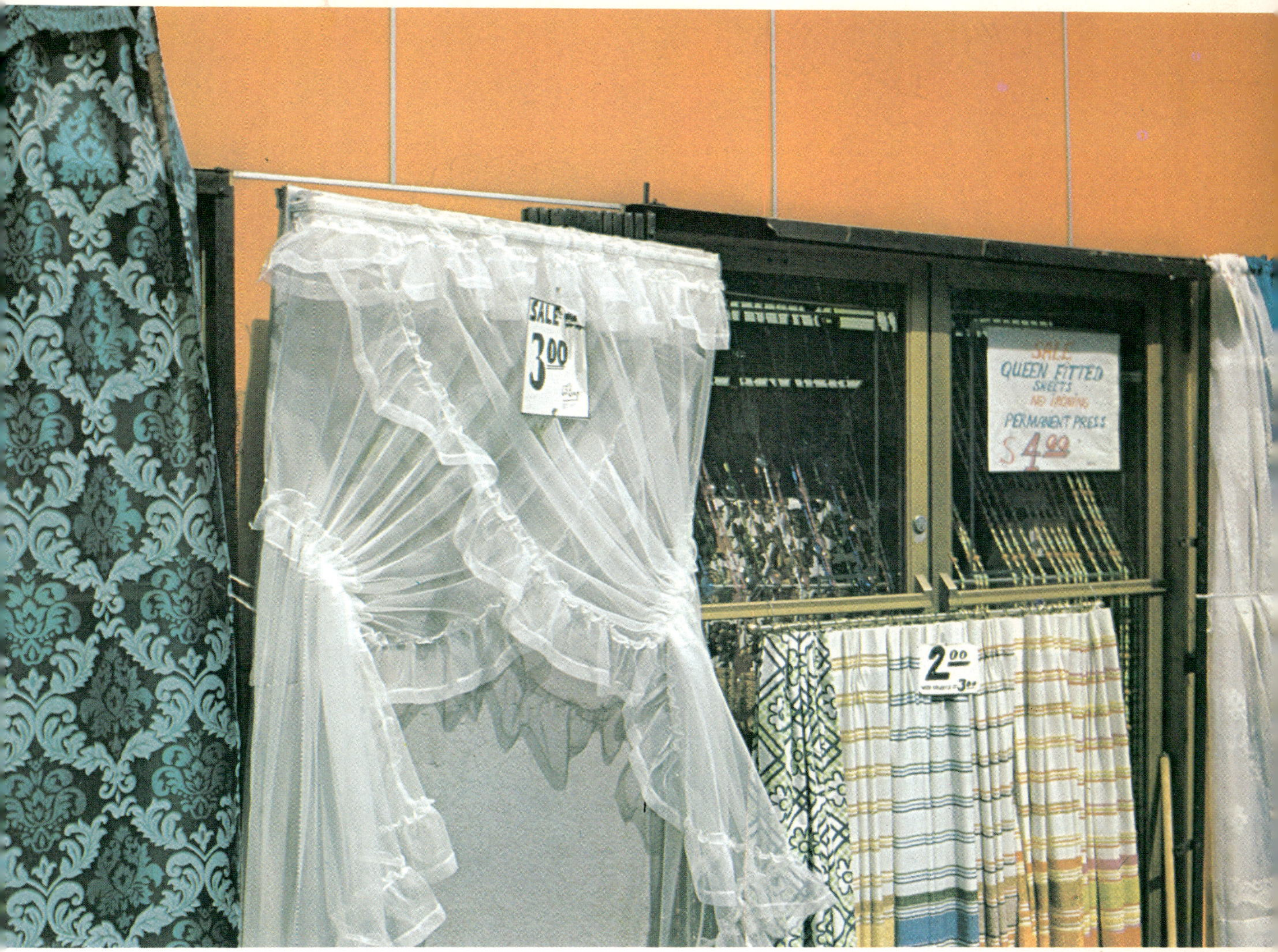

Talking about the color of things relies on a sort of gentlemen's agreement. We call white "white"—morning, noon, or night—despite the fact that the same white object is subject to slight color shifts and variations due to the time of day and the weather. Daylight is reddish at sunrise and sunset and decidedly bluish on rainy or overcast days. Objects illuminated by natural light will show up slightly "off-color" unless filters are used. But, the color shifts apparent in color photography can add to the effect of your shot by contributing a sense of time and weather. The two photos opposite show the bluing effect of moisture in the air. The shot at top was taken on a rainy summer afternoon. The lower shot was taken at pre-dawn following an ice storm. The photo above, taken on Agfachrome film, demonstrates the brilliant color palette of color film used in bright noon sunlight. Here the whites are truly white and the surrounding color of the wall and curtains fully saturated. Photo opposite top by Patricia Maye. Photo opposite bottom by Seymour D. Uslan. Photo above by Raphael Fraguada.

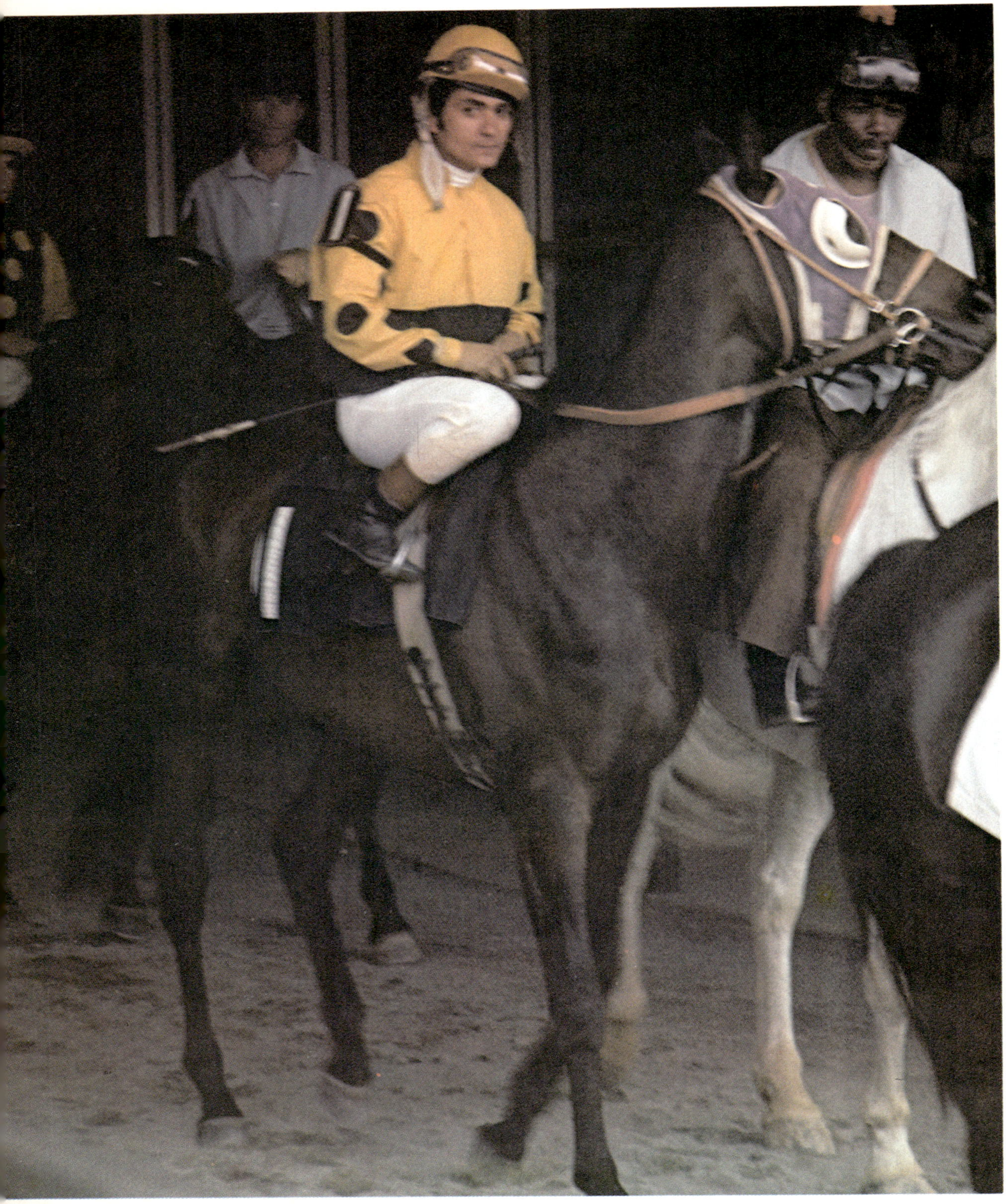

3

CAMERA SETTINGS

Color films have less exposure latitude than black-and-white films. Exposure calculations must be precise. When there is a broad tonal range between the darkest and lightest areas of your view, you, the photographer, must decide where you wish to place the emphasis. In the shot opposite, taken as the horses and riders emerged from the dark passageway under the grandstand at New York's Belmont Park, the shadow areas predominated. The camera's built-in exposure meter gave a reading that would have given detail in the shadows but would have burned out the brightly colored highlights. Thus, the photographer ignored the meter's advice and exposed for the highlights—an underexposure of two stops if the meter was to be accepted. Photo by Patricia Maye.

SETTING YOUR CAMERA

Any camera—from the cheapest and simplest through the most expensive and complicated—is simply a lighttight box with a hole to admit light and a mechanism to control the time during which the light is admitted. Simple box cameras feature a standard-sized hole and a standard time exposure that allow for taking pictures in normal light conditions. Adjustable cameras, such as the great variety of 35mm models now available, allow the photographer to adjust the size of the light-admitting hole and the time of the exposure. Thus, they expand the perimeters of his picture taking by permitting him to shoot in other than normal light conditions, at other than standard shutter speeds, and to control the pictorial look of his photograph. As complicated as it may seem at first, then, your adjustable camera has only two controls.

F/STOP SETTINGS

Within your lens is a set of overlapping metal leaves called an *iris diaphragm.* The diaphragm can be set to close down or to enlarge the hole through which light enters the camera. The hole is called the *aperture* and its various settings are referred to as *f/stops.* They appear on your lens in a series that runs 2, 2.8, 4, 5.6, 8, 11, 16, 22 plus or minus a setting at either end.

The actual size of the aperture at each *f*/stop is the result of simple mathematics. The equation used is:

$$\frac{1}{f} = \frac{\text{aperture}}{\text{focal length}}$$

Thus, an *f*/stop of 4 on a 50mm lens would mean that at that setting the actual aperture through which light would enter the camera would measure 12.5mm in diameter:

$$\frac{1}{4} = \frac{\text{aperture}}{\text{50mm}}$$

$$\frac{\text{50mm}}{4} = \text{aperture}$$

$$\text{12.5mm} = \text{aperture}$$

Similarly, an *f*/stop of 4 on a 200mm lens would represent an aperture size of 50mm.

Apertures are represented as *f*/stops rather than as real measurements to allow for standardization of exposures. Shots made at *f*/4 with a 50mm lens and at *f*/4 with a 200mm lens at the same shutter speed produce equivalent exposures on the film. The 200mm shot needs a larger physical aperture admitting more light because once admitted the light must travel further down the barrel of the longer lens and its intensity is diminished along the way.

The sequence of the numbers as expressed on your lens may prove baffling at first. You must bear two things in mind in choosing a setting. The first is that, as the equation above shows, the *f*/number is actually the lower part of a fraction. Thus, the larger *f*/numbers represent the smaller openings—just as $^1/_2$ is larger than $^1/_{22}$, *f*/2 will give a larger opening than *f*/22. For the largest opening you must choose the smallest *f*/number on your lens.

The second important fact about *f*/stop settings is that light is entering your lens through a more or less circular opening. The area of the circle, directly related to the amount of light admitted, is determined by squaring its radius (d/2). Thus, if you double the diameter of the circle, you'll quadruple the area of the circle and the amount of light admitted. For example, we discovered earlier that a setting of *f*/4 on a 50mm lens will give an aperture diameter of 12.5mm. We can also find that *f*/2 will give a diameter of 25mm and *f*/8 will give a diameter of 6.25mm. Applying these measurements to the grade school formula—Area= πr^2—we discover that an *f*/2 setting will yield a circle with an area of 156 π, *f*/4 will yield a circle of area 39 π, and *f*/8 will yield a circle of 9.7 π—a nearly exact progression, not of halving the light admitted but of quartering it as we move from *f*/2 to *f*/4 to *f*/8.

The progression of *f*/stops listed above—2, 2.8, 4, 5.6, 8, 11, 16, 22—takes into account this squaring step in finding the circle's area. A move from one to the next in that sequence represents a doubling or halving of the light admitted. Any intermediary numbers found on your lens—*f*/3.5 is often included—represent half stops, necessary for critical and precise intermediary exposures where doubling or halving exposure would not produce the desired effect.

SHUTTER SPEEDS

Your shutter-speed selection determines the duration of your exposure. The shutter-speed dial on your camera indicates the number of seconds and fractions thereof at which your shutter can be made to open and close. The sequence usually runs from 1 or $^1/_2$ second through $^1/_{500}$th or $^1/_{1000}$th second in a direct arithmetical progression. Most of the settings are fractions of seconds (1/shutterspeed). By going from $^1/_{500}$th to $^1/_{1000}$th second you'll cut exposure time in half. The shutter speed is the complement of the aperture. Together, these two settings establish the correct exposure.

WHICH COMBINATION IS CORRECT?

Anyone who has ever used a hand-held light meter will already know that for any given light situation many complementary aperture and shutter-speed combinations will yield a correct exposure. When you bring the needle in a through-the-lens light meter into alignment with the marker you are selecting only one of these combinations.

Suppose your camera's shutter is set at 1/125th sec. and you are metering through the lens by closing down your aperture. The needle might come into correct exposure position when your lens setting reaches *f*/11. Shoot and you'll get a picture.

A hand-held meter, on the other hand, measuring the same light conditions would indicate a range of correct picture-making exposures. You would surely find *f*/11 at 1/125th sec. indicated, but there would also be *f*/8 at 1/250th, *f*/5.6 at 1/500th, and so on up and down the aperture and shutter-speed dials. What would be apparent is that if you go to a higher shutter-speed setting for a faster exposure you must balance the decrease in exposure time—and thus the decrease in the amount of light hitting the film—by increasing the size of the aperture. Conversely, if you choose a small aperture, you must balance it with a longer exposure time.

Choosing a combination of shutter speed and aperture is much more than a matter of correct exposure. A photo taken with a fast shutter and large lens aperture will prove very different from one taken with a slow shutter speed and small aperture although the exposures for both would be correct. Shoot off a roll on your own to prove the point or refer to the landscape shots on pages 42-43 that we have included to demonstrate the differences. The following text sections discuss the changes that are apparent in such a set of pictures.

In terms of exposure many *f*/stop—shutter-speed combinations are correct for any given light situation. The photo of the landscape at right was taken at a setting of *f*/8 with the appropriate complementary shutter-speed setting. The differences produced by different *f*/stop settings is apparent in the photos on the following pages. The seemingly soft or out of focus picture on the left (page 42) is, in truth, in focus. Note the sharply defined branch and leaves at the top of the frame. The camera was focused on that branch. Because of a *f*/stop setting of *f*/4 little else is in focus. The picture on the right (page 43) is also sharply focused on the branch. But, in this case, much more of the scene is rendered in sharp focus. For this shot, a *f*/ setting of *f*/16 was used. Photos by Rafael Fraguada.

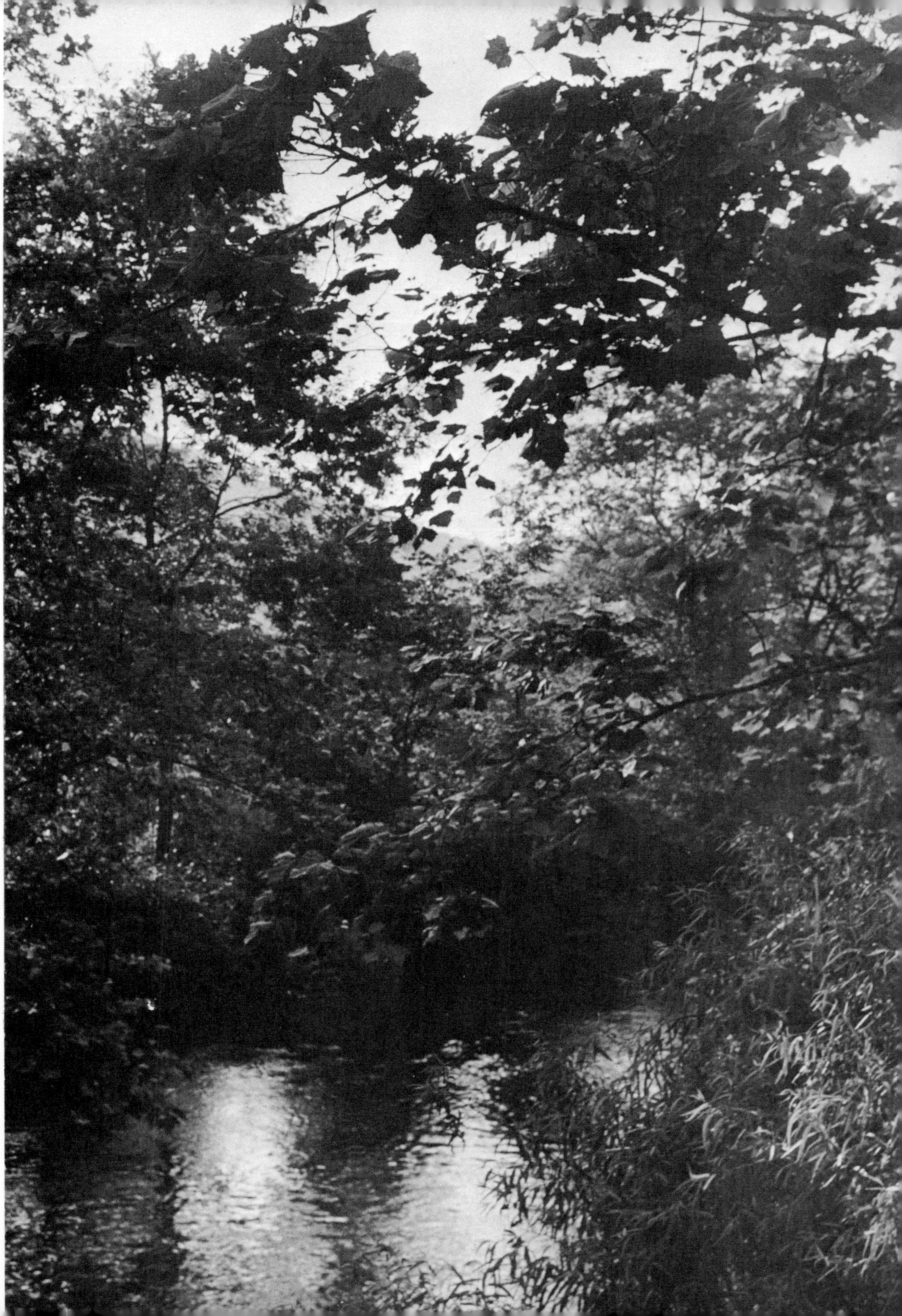

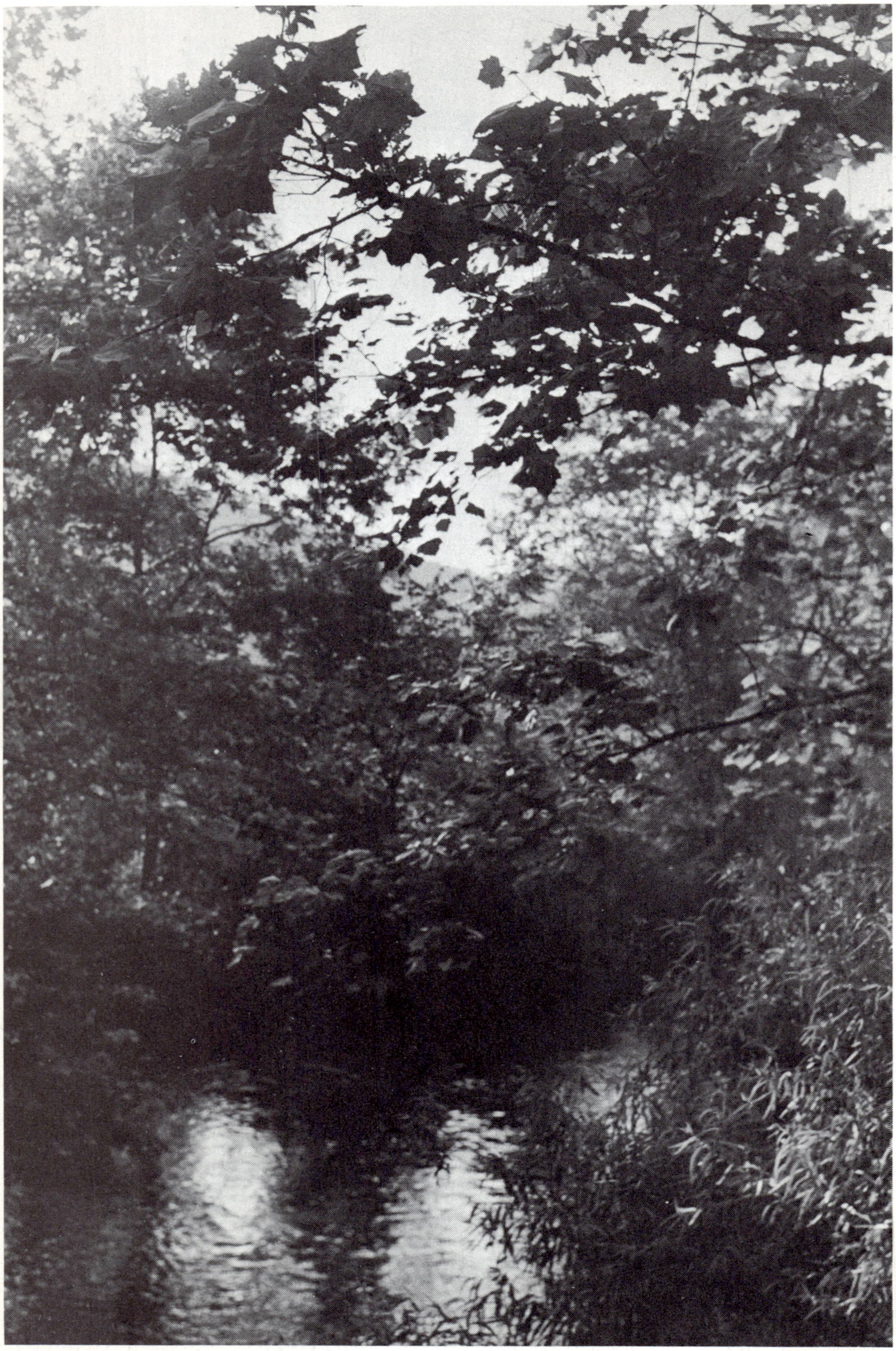

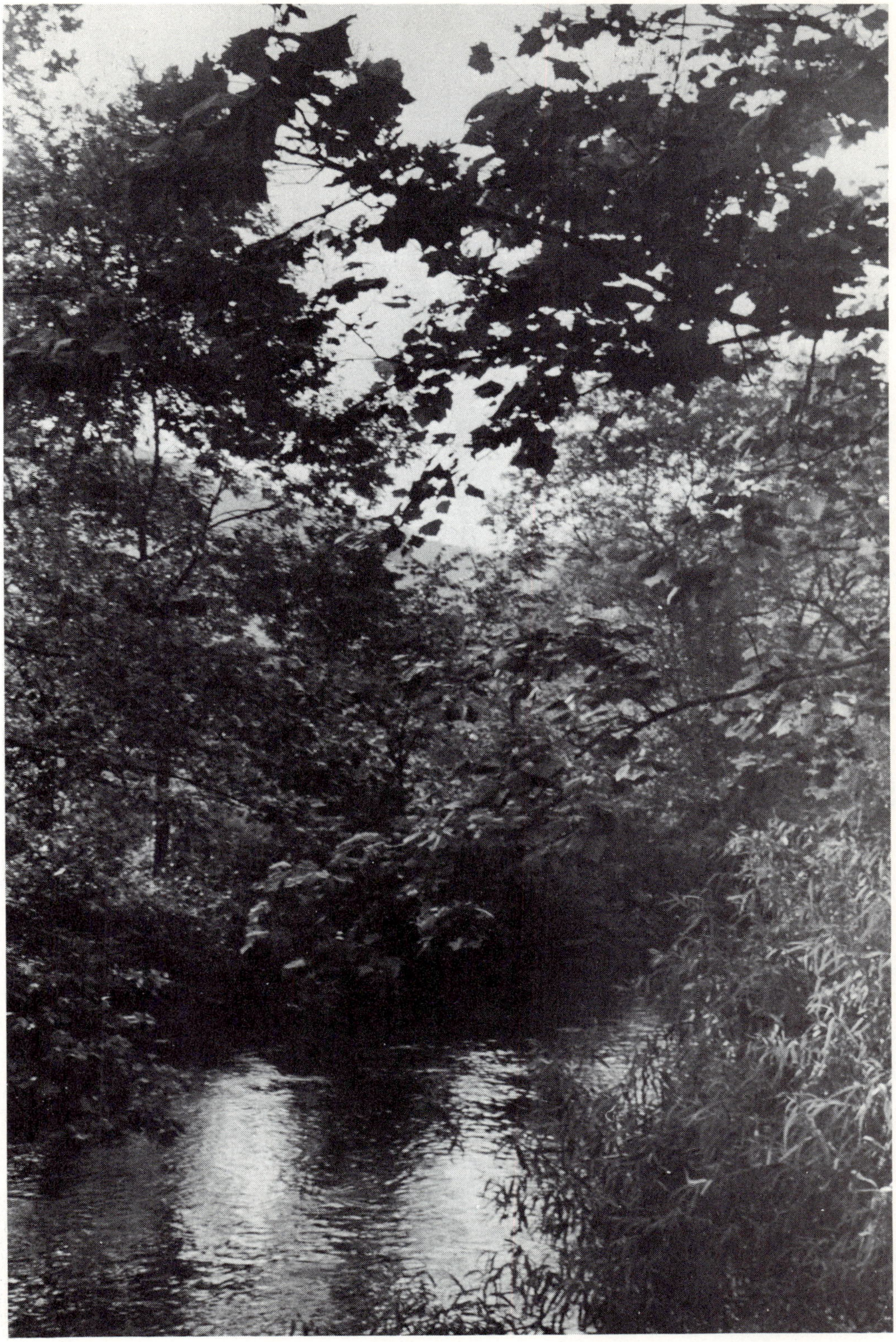

SHUTTER SPEED—FAST OR SLOW?

The speed of whatever action or subject you are shooting is the prime consideration in choosing a shutter speed. Shooting sports, dance, or any fast moving subject naturally requires a fast shutter to freeze the action. But, the speed of your subject's motion must be considered in relation to the camera-to-subject distance. A man running across a field in the far distance of a landscape shot can be easily frozen at $^1/_{100}$th or $^1/_{125}$th sec. A man running across the near foreground at the same rate of speed would require a shutter speed of $^1/_{1000}$th sec. to be rendered clearly.

The direction of the subject's motion must also be taken into account. Action moving directly toward or away from the camera merely grows in size in your viewer and on your film. A subject moving parallel to the camera—across the field of view—is displaced much more in the viewer and on the film and will be blurred and will require a faster shutter speed than the oncoming or withdrawing subject. Thus, subject speed, the camera-to-subject distance, and the direction of travel all come into play in choosing an action-stopping shutter speed.

Action stopping is not always the basis for choosing a shutter speed, however. Occasionally, you may wish to deliberately blur an action shot. Or, more often, with static or posed subjects, the *f*/stop will become your main concern and the shutter speed will be chosen as a complement to it.

When the subject is well illuminated, the shutter speed can be considered primarily as an action stopper. Both the action shots opposite were taken at high shutter speeds to freeze the subject. Both shots were also taken at what is called the "peak of action"—the split second at which an upward-bound object stops just before starting its downward course. The combination of a fast shutter and peak of action shooting is part of every action photographer's bag of tricks. Photo opposite top by Horst Schafer. Photo opposite below by Daniel Rubin/Photo Trends.

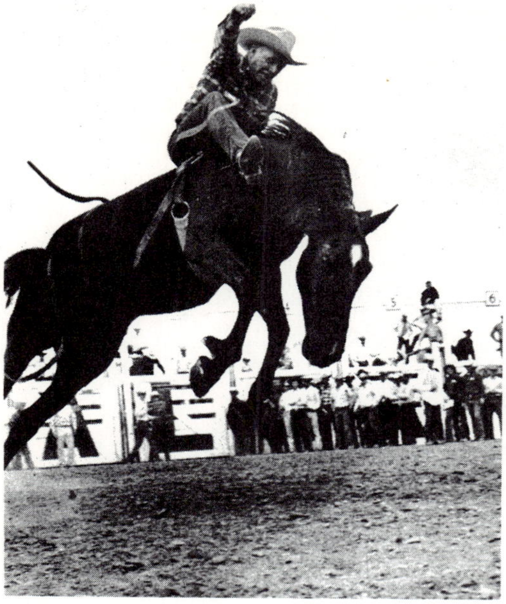

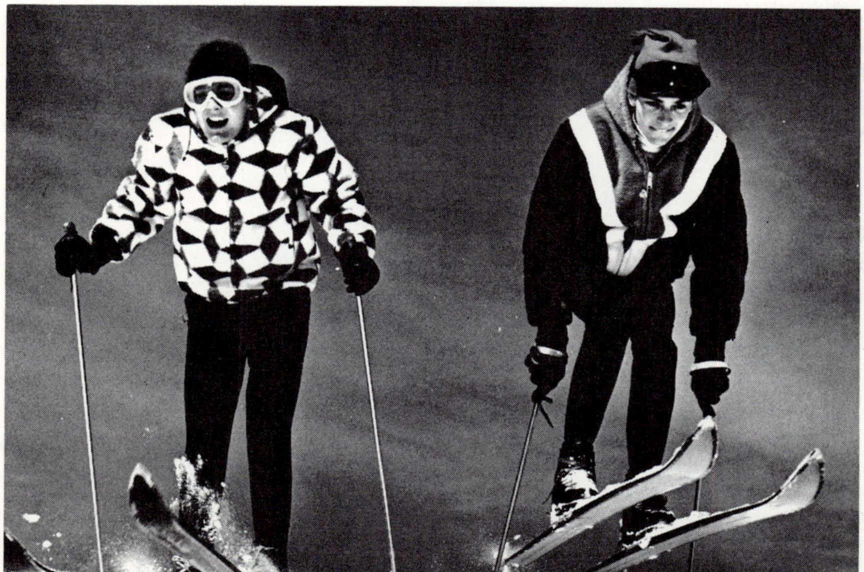

CHOOSING AN *f*/STOP

In shots where action stopping is not of chief interest, the choice of your *f*/stop will be a matter of what sort of look you wish your picture to have. As the landscape series taken at the various *f*/stop and shutter-speed combinations shows, the area of your picture rendered in acceptable focus varies with the *f*/stop in use. Small apertures (high *f*/numbers) yield photos with a great deal of in-focus area. Large apertures (small f/numbers) give pictures with a shallow in-focus area.

DEPTH OF FIELD

The zone of sharpness in your picture is called the depth of field. Its limits depend on three factors—the *f*/stop setting, the distance focused on, and the focal length of the lens in use.

Small apertures yield generous depths of field; depth of field diminishes when the camera is focused on a close subject; and, long focal length lenses have substantially less depth of field at any given *f*/stop and focusing distance than a normal lens focused at the same distance and set at the same f/stop, while short focal length lenses have more.

When shooting any subject and thinking photographically, it's up to you to decide how much or little around your prime subject you wish to have in focus. A portrait of a subject posed a few feet in front of a distracting or unattractive background might well call for a large aperture, a closer focusing distance, or a longer focal length lens to throw the background out of focus. An overall, interesting subject—a garden party or group activity, say—might demand a depth of field as deep as possible, achieved by setting on a small aperture, backing off from the subject, or by using a short focal-length lens.

Always remember to readjust your shutter speed to offset increases or decreases in aperture size. In reading off a hand-held meter choose the smallest-aperture–longest-shutter-speed combination for maximum depth of field or the largest-aperture–fastest-shutter combination for minimum depth of field. If your camera has a built-in meter, set the shutter speed at the lowest setting practical for the subject motion and then stop the lens down to the smallest practical aperture for maximum depth of field. Or, choose the fastest shutter speed your camera offers then open the lens up to limit the depth of field.

Considering your *f*/stop as more than an exposure factor will give you control over the all-important depth of field, which you will soon discover is one of the primary creative tools of the thinking photographer.

Depth of field was deliberately curtailed in the photo below. The normal 58mm lens was opened up to maximum aperture and focus was placed on the close foreground grasses. The large aperture and short focusing distance combined to hold the depth of field to a minimum and throw the background face entirely out of focus for an impressionistic effect. Photo by Rafael Fraguada.

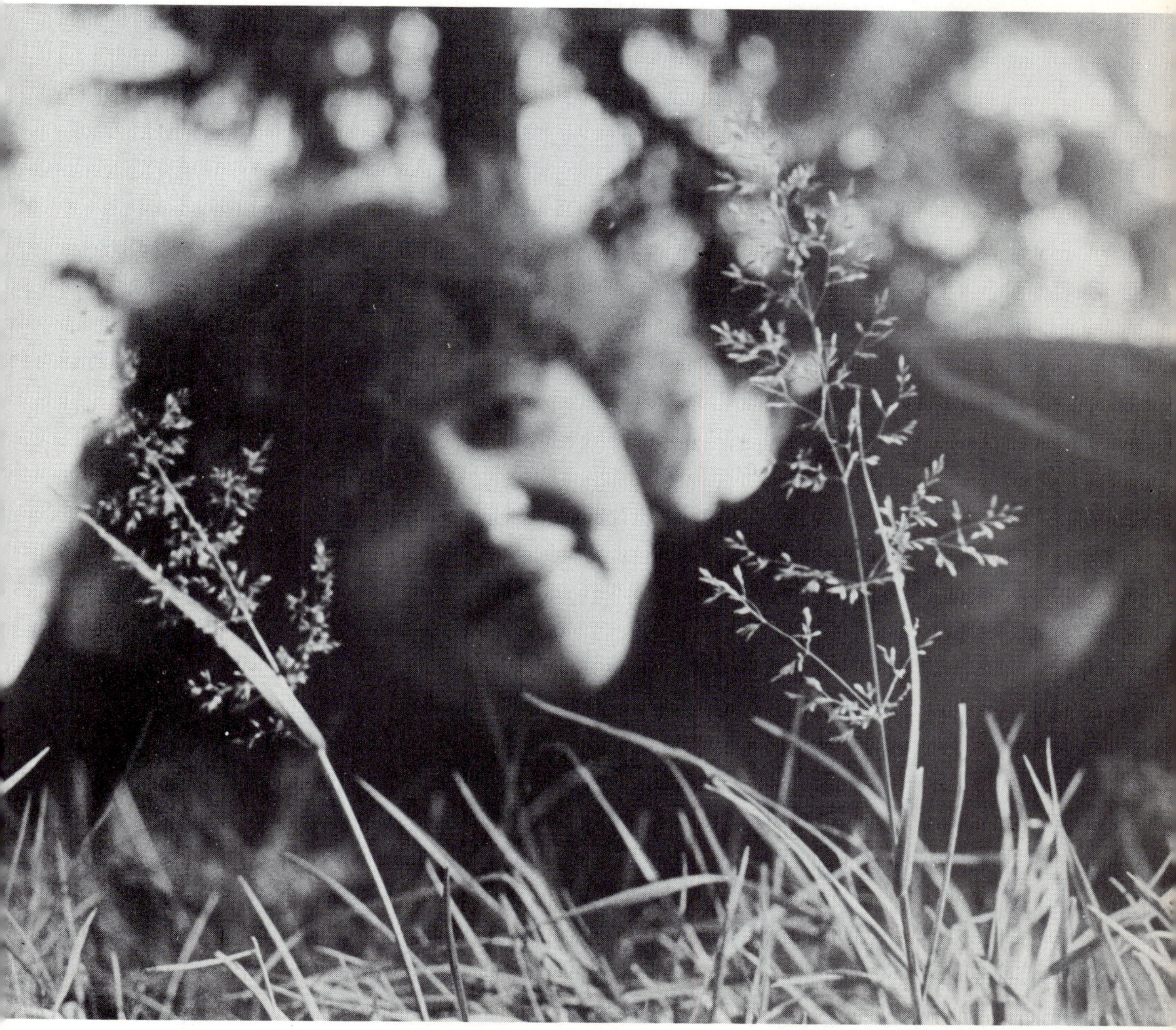

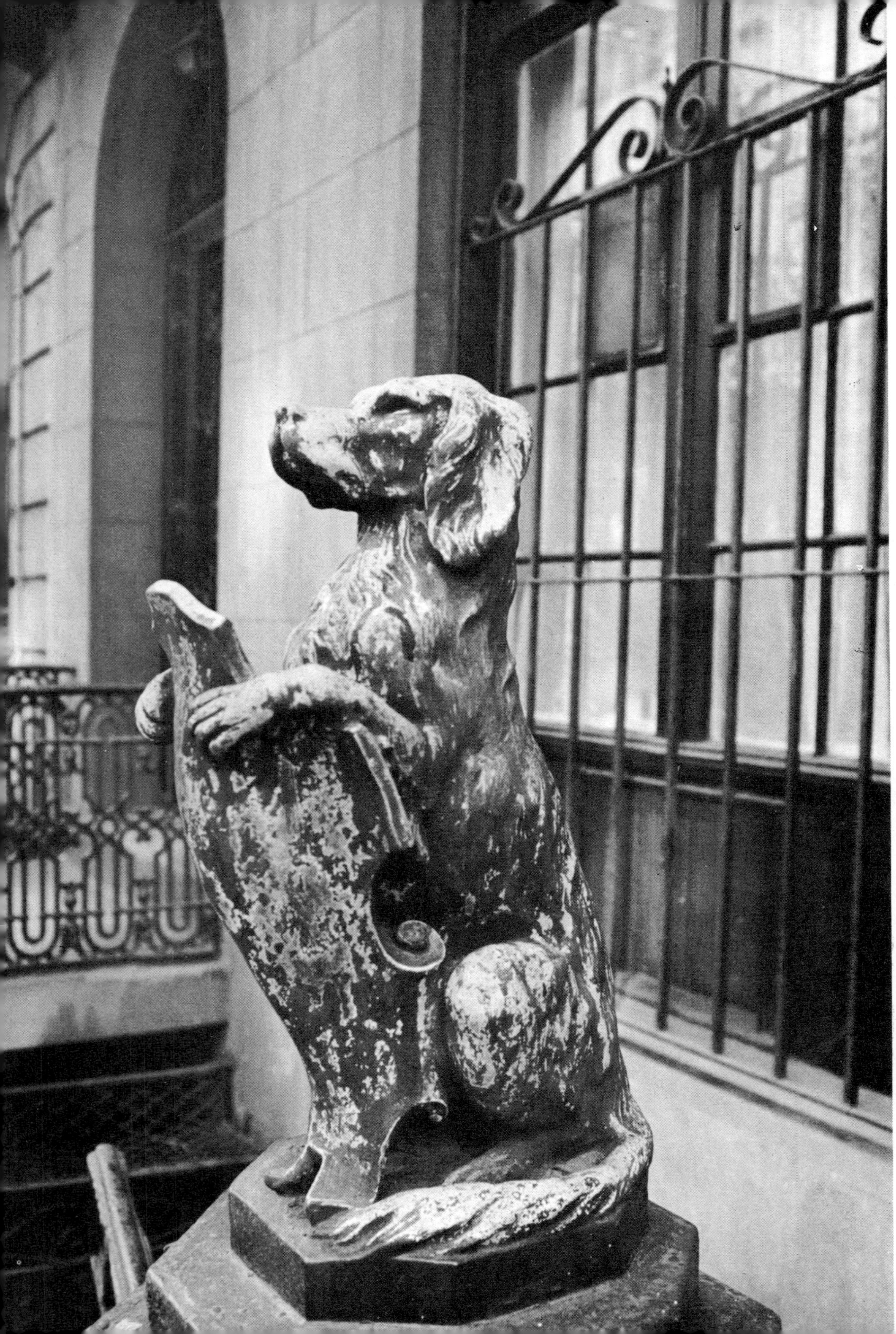

The inverse proportion between depth of field and focal length is demonstrated in these two photos. The sculpted dog at left was photographed with a 35mm lens. The shorter-than-normal lens offered a good depth of field—enough to include the details of the background architecture and iron work. The real dog below was photographed from across the yard with a 135mm lens. The in-focus area is restricted to the dog alone. The background bushes become a soft shadowy pattern. Photo opposite by Rafael Fraguada. Photo below by Patricia Maye.

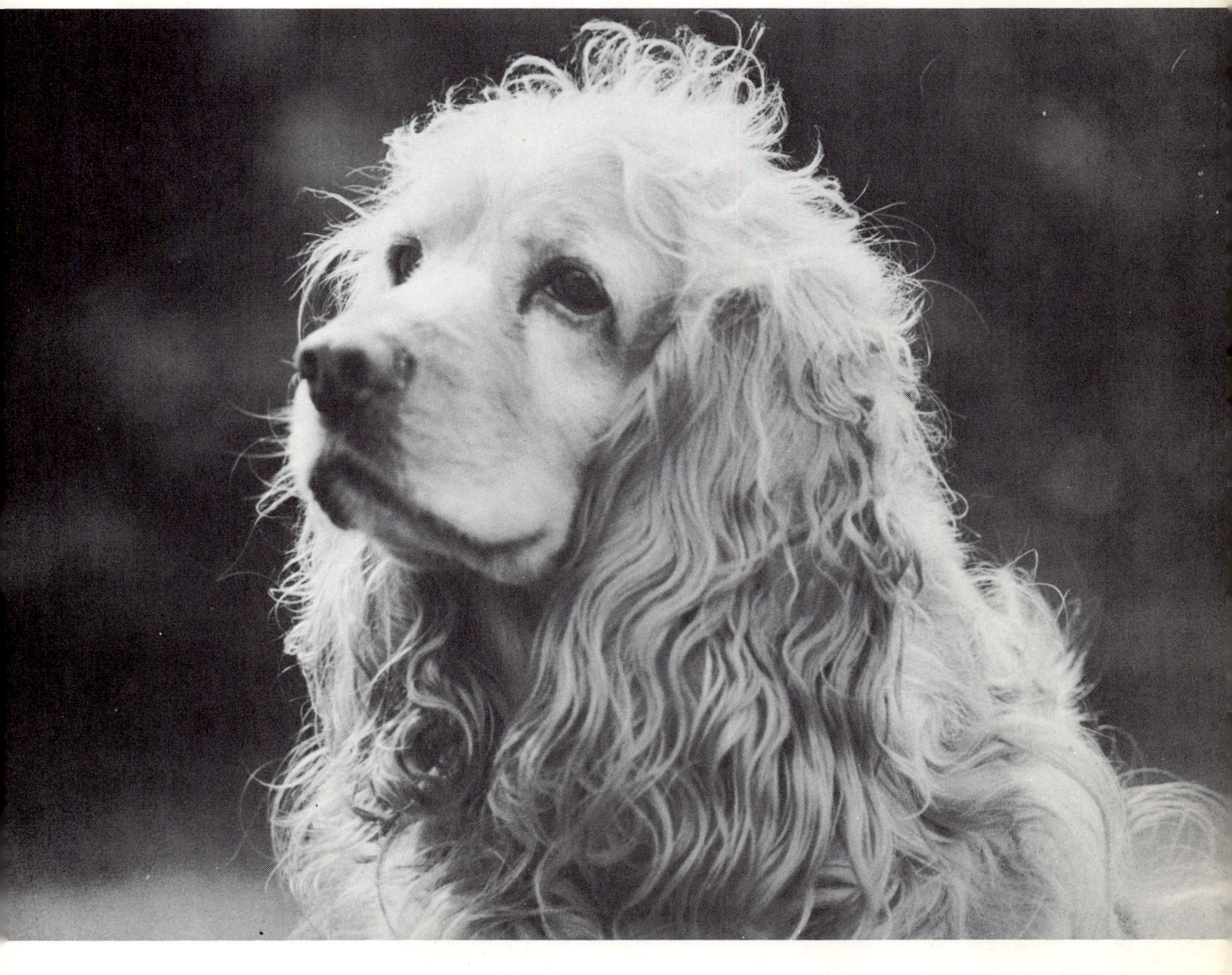

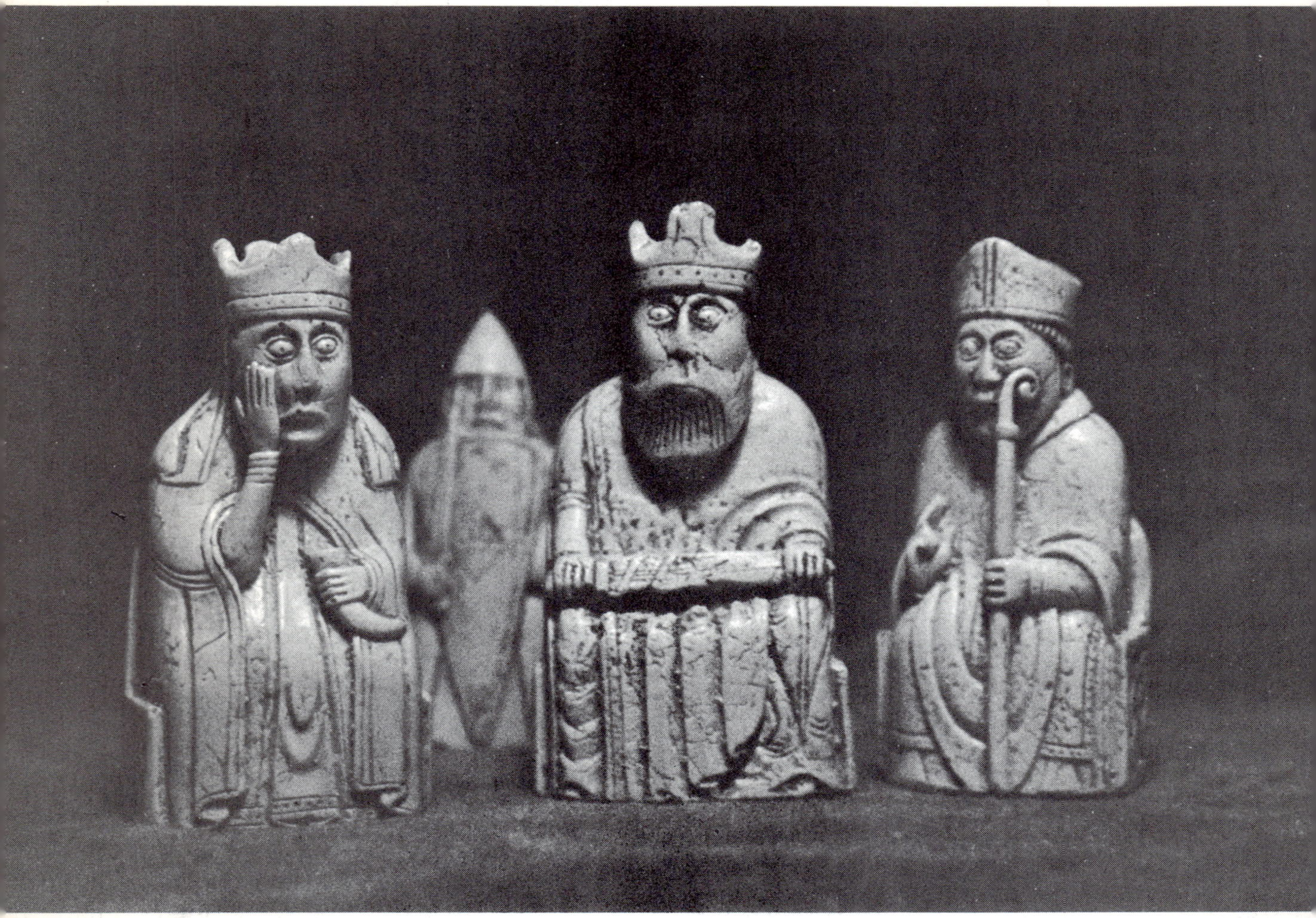

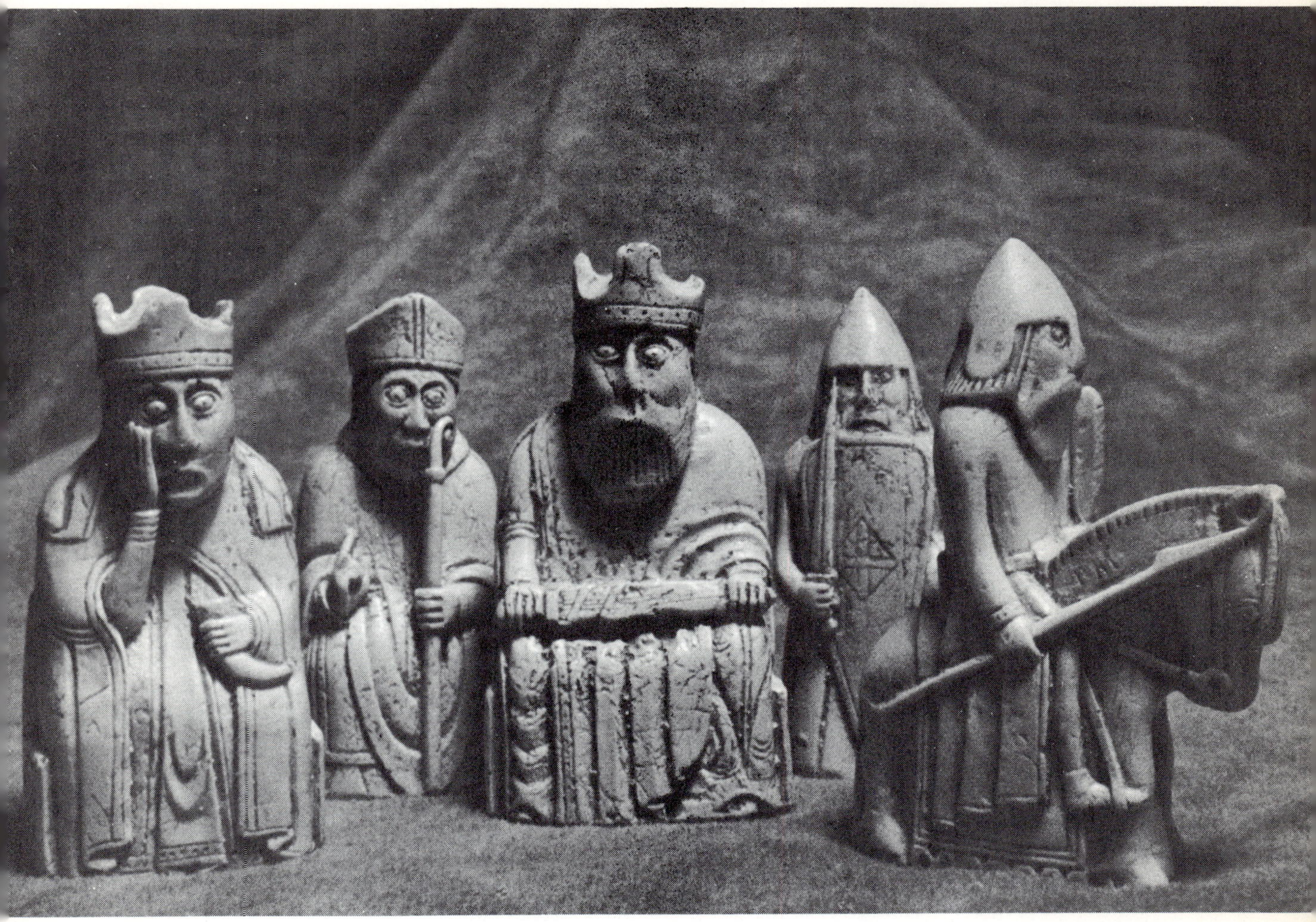

The depth of field of any lens is shallowest when the lens is focused on a close subject. The chess pieces on these pages were photographed with a 35mm lens from about 2 feet away. The photo at left was taken by the available light of an overhead lamp at an aperture of *f*/2.8. When a photoflood lamp was added to provide extra illumination a smaller *f*/stop—*f*/8—could be used and the depth of field was enhanced somewhat. Photos by Patricia Maye.

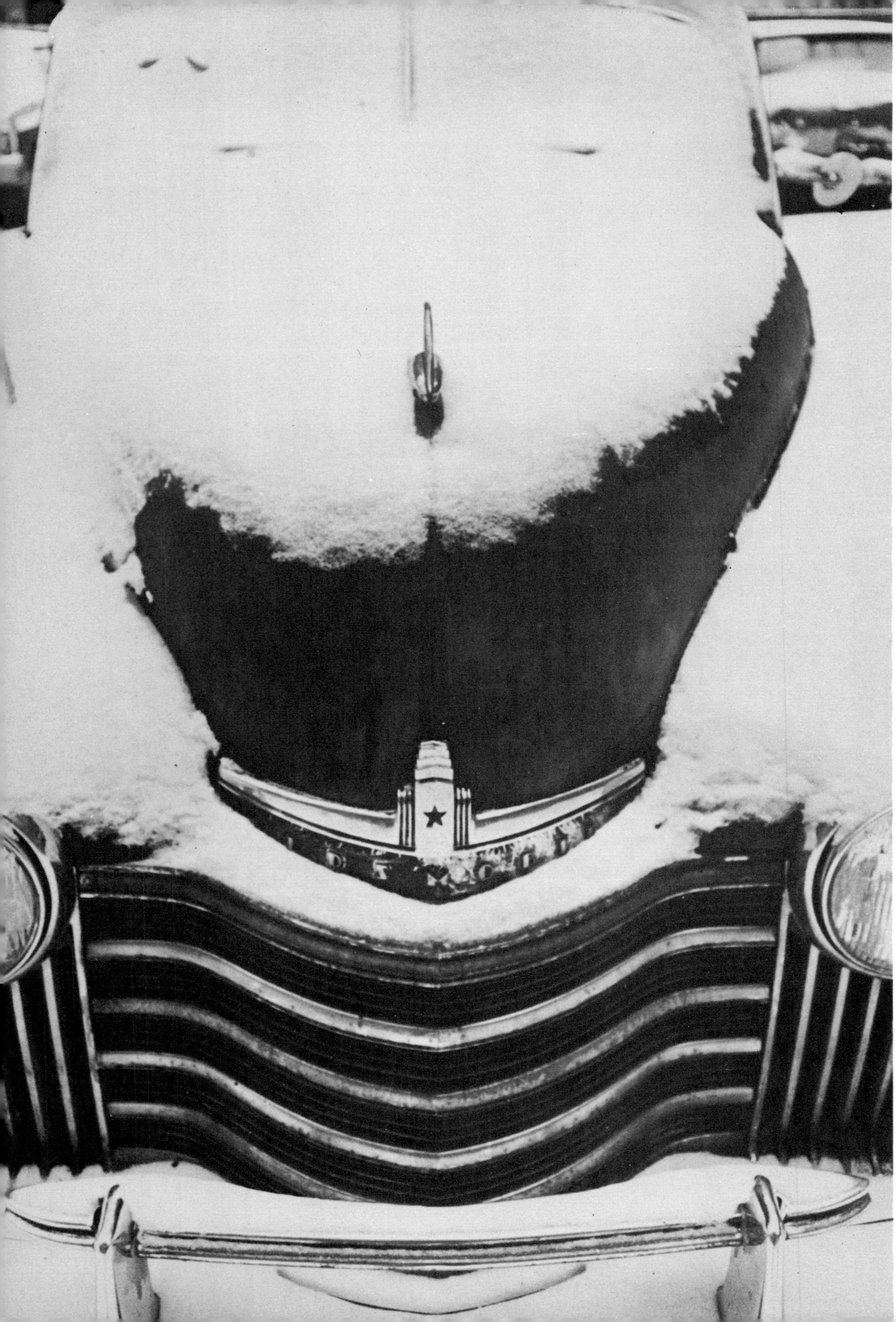

4

THE CREATIVE PHOTOGRAPHER

The "creative" photographer is ever on the lookout for subjects for his camera. This snow covered car seemed to have been transformed into a mechanical monster by the weather. Photo by Rafael Fraguada.

THE CREATIVE PHOTOGRAPHER

If your original enthusiasm for photography has dampened, it is easy to revert to a process known as "letting the camera collect dust." This condition is one in which we find the once-cherished object closeted away, pining for action, only to see the light of day (or night) when its once-eager owner wants to snap a few record shots: his child's seventh birthday party, his daughter's first formal, or a reunion with an old war buddy. Inaction is a terrible disease for a camera, especially since it was promised so much by the manufacturer; lack of enthusiasm by the photographer for an instrument which has so much to offer him is equally sad.

Here's a remedy!

Once you've progressed from the functional aspects of learning how to use your equipment and take successful snapshots, there are many creative camera techniques for you to experiment with and enjoy. You will also enjoy the pictures that you will achieve with them.

If your interest in photography has wilted, perhaps the pages that follow will pep up your spirits; if you are still enamored, they may add even more spice to your hobby.

SEEING CREATIVELY

Vision is a habit we take for granted, and so we often tend to miss seeing many of the beautiful things around us. If they register on our retinas we pass quickly on to another image, and give them no more than a passing thought, or, more likely, no thought at all.

Many non-photographers are unaware of the shapes and sizes and textures and colors of things. They never consciously notice the different nuances in lighting, the marvelous reflections and shadows. But once they take a look at the world through a view-finder they begin to notice all sorts of wonderful sights. Finally, they need not look through a camera to see them, but photography was the passport to this new perception.

Developing the ability to see creatively enables you to take the ordinary and give it your own interpretation, which is what will make your picture come alive.

Seeing creatively involves many aspects of photography: it supplies the reasons why you select a particular location and model—why you choose a particular angle and form of lighting—why you pick a particular shot to enlarge and why you crop and print it in a particular way.

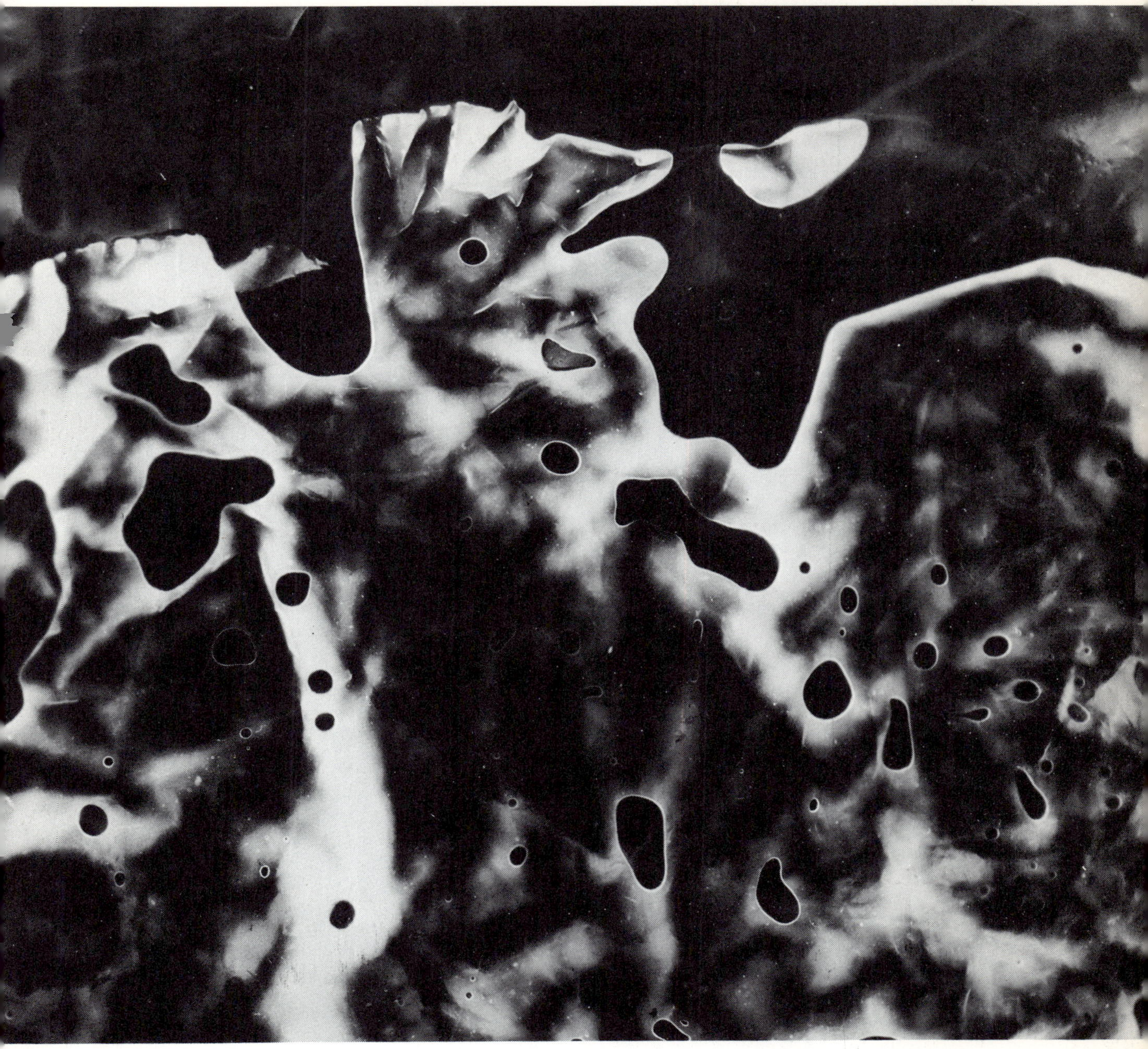

Photography literally means "light drawing". The camera is usually considered an inherent part of the photographic process, but photographs can be produced without a subject, camera, or film. The image above—a gluttonous bird in the thinking of the photographer—was produced by placing some crumpled wax paper on top of enlarging paper then exposing the two to light. Such "photograms" can stand by themselves or produce interesting textures to combine with your conventional photographs. Photogram by Patricia Maye.

CHOICE OF SUBJECT MATTER

One of the differences between the ordinary amateur and the creative photographer is the conversation which takes place within him before he takes a picture. Usually the amateur's goes something like: "There's the U.N. I'll take a picture." And he snaps his camera to his nose, focuses and clicks.

The creative photographer's conversation is somewhat longer and more meaningful. "I'd like to take a picture of the U.N., but I don't want the usual postcard type. Let's see where the best angle of view is." Then he remembers some skyscrapers several blocks away. "Since it's late afternoon I might be able to get their reflections in the glass windows of the U.N." He crosses the street and sees them. But the picture is still not just right. "It should have people in it doing something; after all, hundreds of people from all over the world visit the U.N. every day." And so he determines his meter reading, sets his speed and lens opening to insure sharpness in the areas he wants and sits down to wait. Pretty soon a policeman wanders into view and rests for a moment, looking at the building. Then a tourist hails the policeman to ask a question. "Great," thinks the photographer and he raises the camera (already prefocused) and takes the picture at the exact instant he wants. There's no need to explain who gets the more interesting shot.

The choice of subject matter (and its final interpretation in the darkroom) is the first consideration in photography. After all, you've got to have a subject to have a picture. Each picture needs a point of focus, and usually needs something prominent in the foreground or background (an object, person, or color) to hold the picture together.

When it comes to subjects like people or animals, many photographers pose them in meaningless positions. The action in a picture has *got* to be believable. Pictures of animals dressed up in clothing, posed talking on telephones are generally repellent—where would you ever see that going on in real life?

Often in your choice of subject matter the time of day (or the artificial lighting you choose) makes a picture become more exciting. Unusual lighting always creates a mood effect. If your street looks too ordinary in daylight to make an interesting subject—go back and look at it at dawn, or at night.

Or you may wish to subordinate the main subject of the shot to some foreground or background detail for a novel effect. Such selective focusing is demonstrated in the photos on pages 46-51.

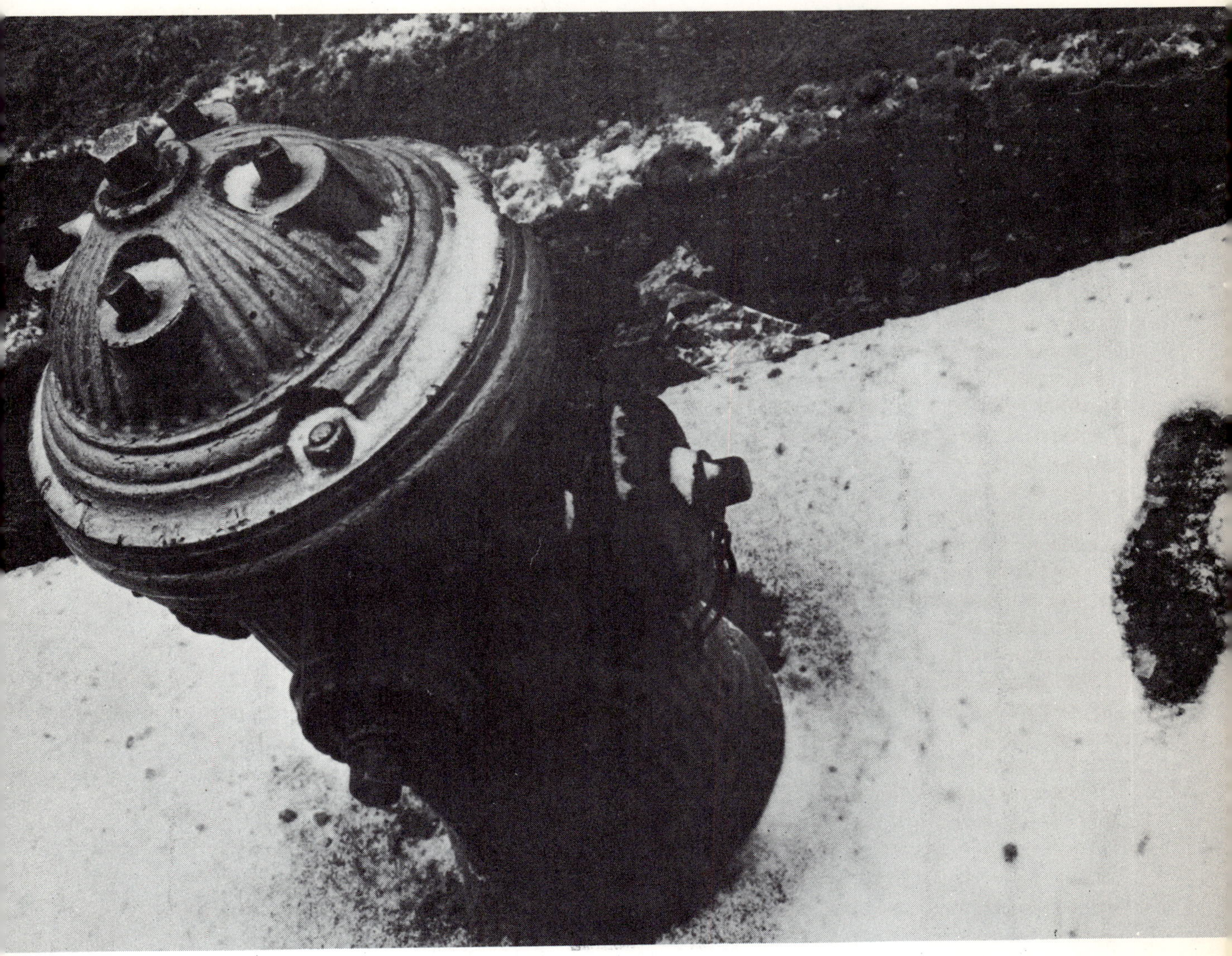

Photography is sometimes the subject of a photograph. The arrangement of dark shapes—the fireplug and footprint—against the light snow is the sole subject of the picture above. Photo by Rafael Fraguada.

KEEP SHOOTING

As all 35mm photographers know, one of the great advantages of the camera is that you can shoot up to 36 frames per roll; you can shoot many times before you need to reload. But although this innovation was created by the manufacturers as an attraction, it has brought confusion to many amateurs. At one extreme is the person who thinks 36 exposures equals 36 different pictures; at the other, the individual who thinks of 36 exposures as equalling a single picture. Somewhere in the middle lies the true answer.

The ease of handling your 35mm camera makes it possible to get several pictures of a subject, insuring that you will get at least one which will please you. Take more than one frame of a single subject—from a different angle or at a different exposure setting. You'll soon learn that your insurance shot or the one that was taken as an after thought is your choice shot for printing and enlarging. Two exposures equal one picture in many a case.

Try presetting your camera so that you will always be ready for that "perfect" picture. Take an exposure meter reading, determine the general area you want in focus, then preset the diaphragm and footage scale. With a 35mm lens set at *f*/8 and 15 feet on the distance scale, for example, everything from eight feet to infinity will be in focus. At *f*/5.6 and 15 feet on the distance scale, everything from about nine feet to 42 feet will be in focus. The shutter speed is then adjusted to the existing light.

Presetting (or zone focusing as it is sometimes called) allows you to advance the film, sight the picture and shoot in rapid sequence. Instruction books for your equipment will provide you with scales for each lens focal length, giving areas of sharpness at different lens openings and distances. If you memorize one or two of these zones of focus for each lens you work with, they will cover most of your shooting situations. Also consult your camera manual on how to use the depth of field scale engraved on the lens.

Never skimp on film. When you find a subject that interests you, risk overshooting rather than missing *the* picture. The photos at right were taken on the tail end of the second roll of film devoted to the subject that day. The photo of the little boy eating his hamburger seemed to wrap the day up with a detail shot from the backyard barbeque. Then, the subject reacted to his father's cooking and the photographer got a very telling shot. Photos by Patricia Maye.

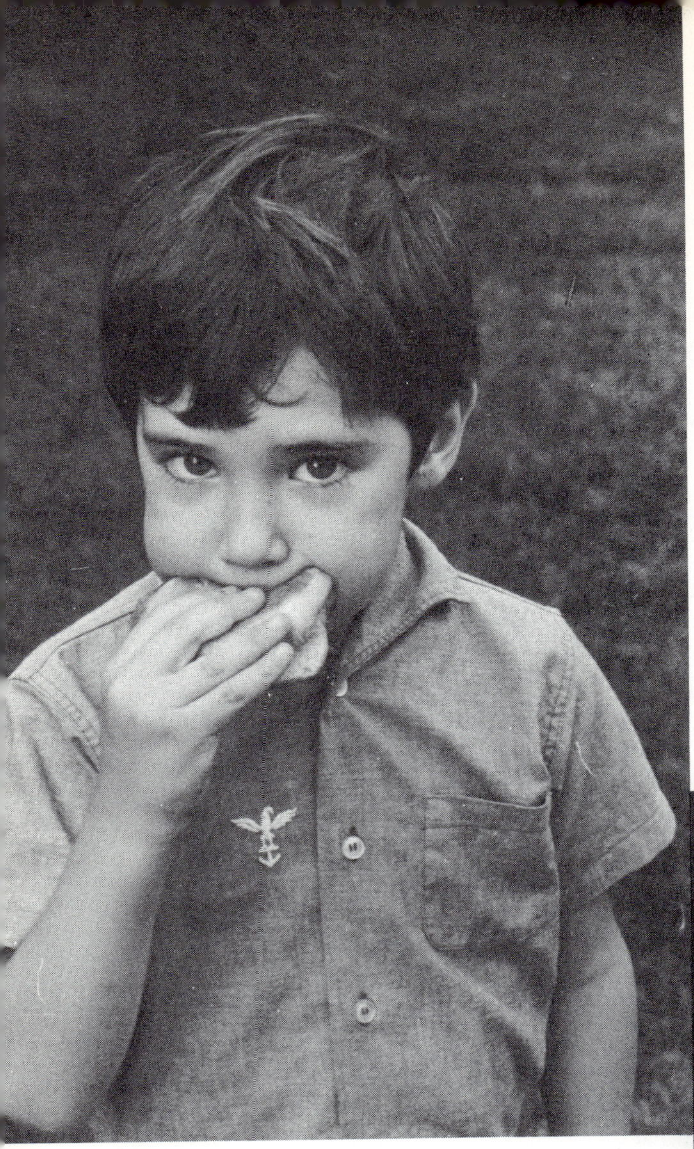
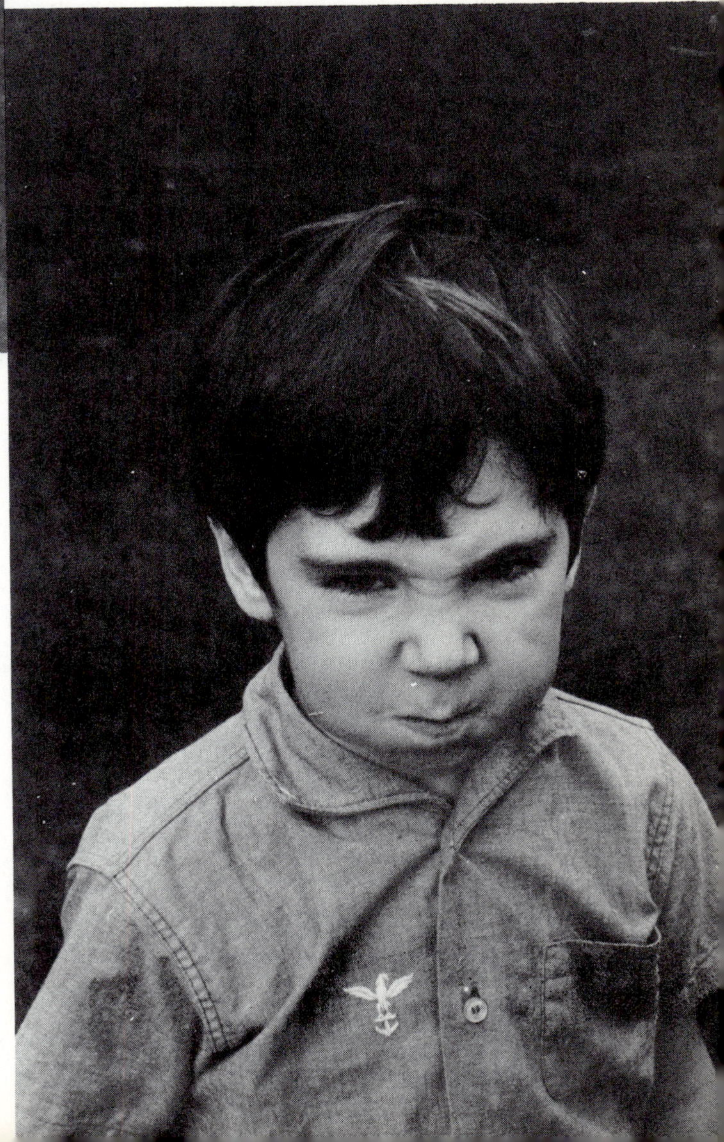

COMPOSITION

Your photographic self-expression is displayed not only by the subject matter you choose to photograph, but also by the way in which you arrange this subject matter within your picture. The meaningful arrangement of the parts of your picture to make a visually satisfying whole is the art of composition.

Well composed photographs are first dictated by their purpose, *i.e.*, a strong or forceful effect can be gained through the use of diagonal lines and unequal masses; a calm effect through perfect balance, which provides a restful composition within the picture.

One of the most important functions of composition is to hold the picture together, but in addition to this, and equally important, is its function of creating a mood which expresses the photographer's feelings about the subject matter. In the picture on page 61 the feeling the photographer wished to express was that of protection. Rounding a corner one day she saw a kitten dash out into the traffic and a pedestrian dart out to save it. A waiter from a nearby restaurant also felt compassion for the lost kitten and brought out a plate of food. The two men stood guard while the kitten ate. This is the mood the photographer tried to capture by composing the picture with the kitten as the point of interest and its two protectors standing strong on either side.

There are several compositional errors to which the beginning photographer often falls victim. One of the most common is forgetting that similar tones and objects will blend together in any photograph—especially in black and white. When this happens we get trees growing out of people's backs and heads.

Another error often committed is that of having more than one point of interest in a picture. This tends to make the picture fall apart and to confuse the person who is trying to admire your work. It is usually better to focus attention on one thing and subordinate everything else.

Pictures which are divided into two equal parts are often badly composed. If you put the thing you want to center interest upon slightly to the right or left, or slightly higher or lower than dead center, you will generally have a more vital and interesting picture.

Having said "don't do these things," we must reverse that position and add—rules are made only to be broken. It is true that good composition can be ruined by committing certain errors, but there are times, and you can only find them through experimentation, when a great composition will result from breaking a few rules!

The composition of the photo at right occurred naturally. Both the straw-hatted waiter and the passerby were interested in the little stray cat and things fell into place without any posing or deliberate composing—Serendipity. Photo by Kathy Wersen.

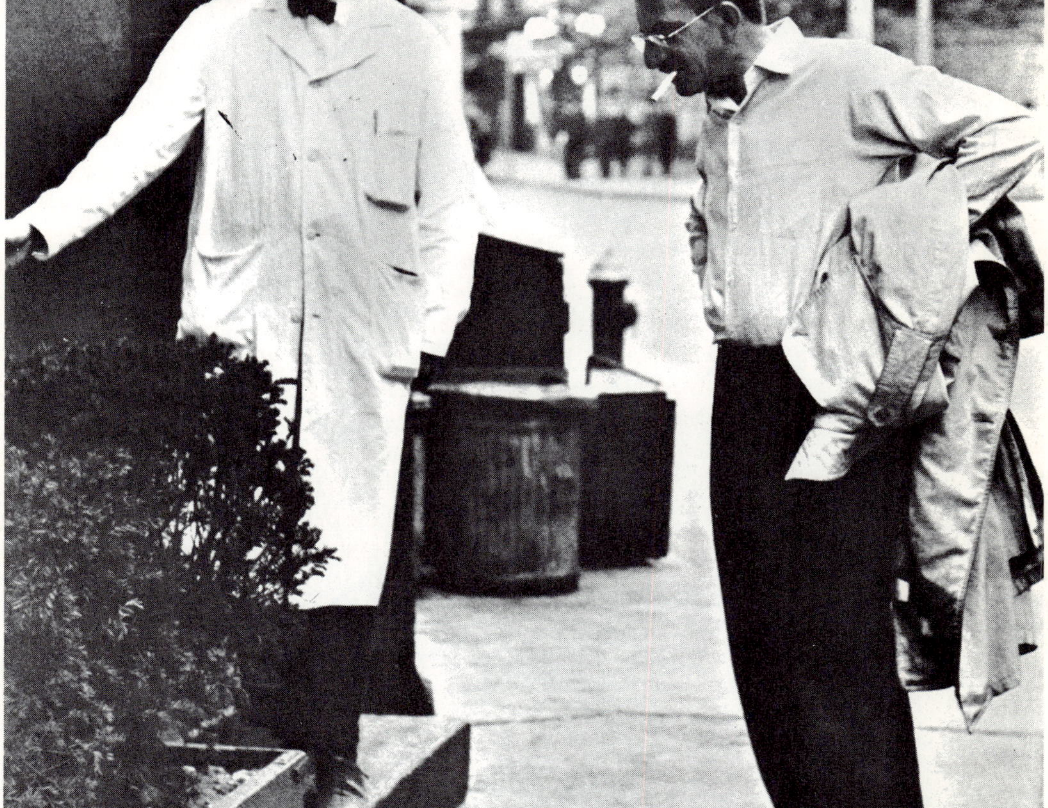

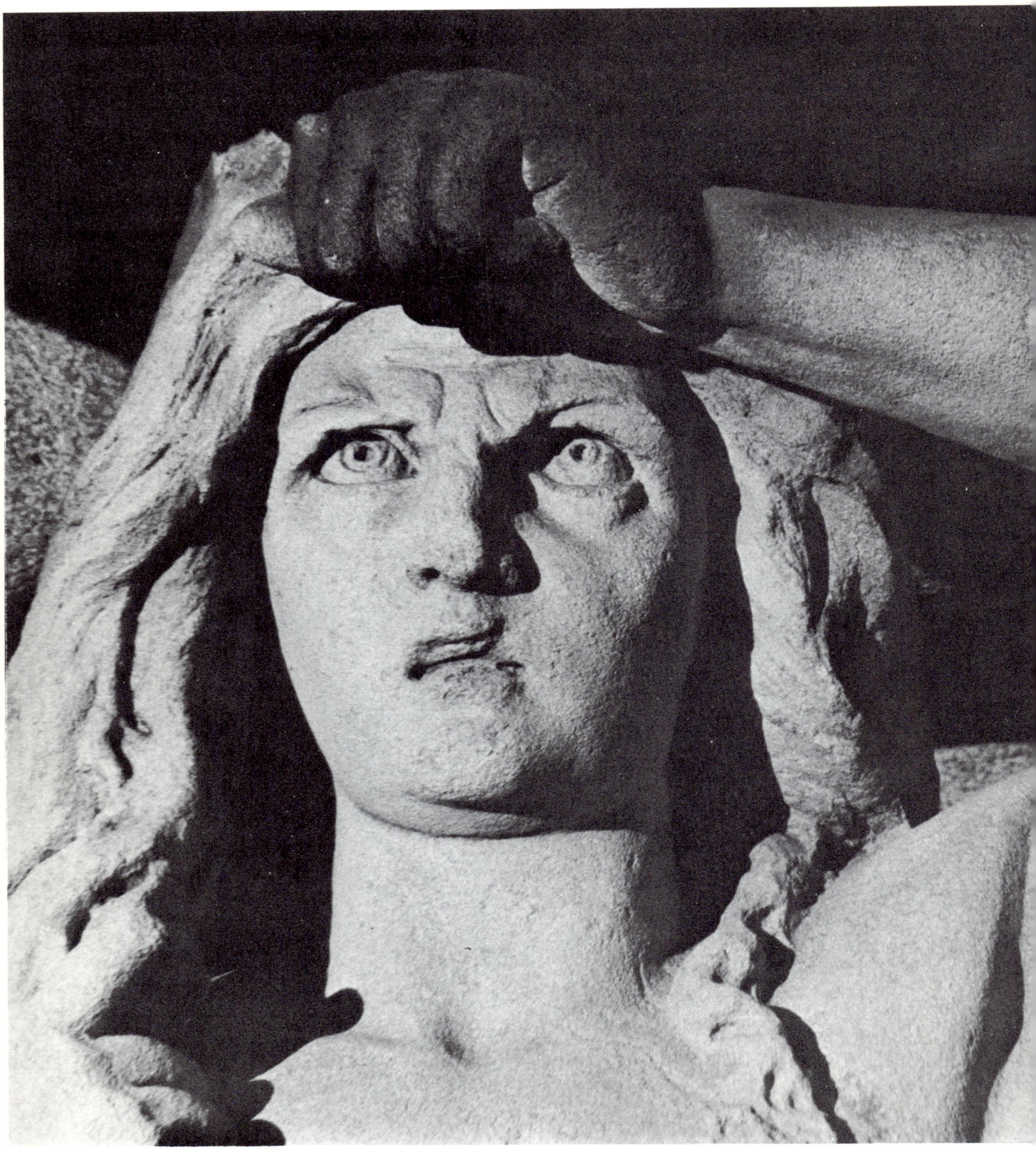

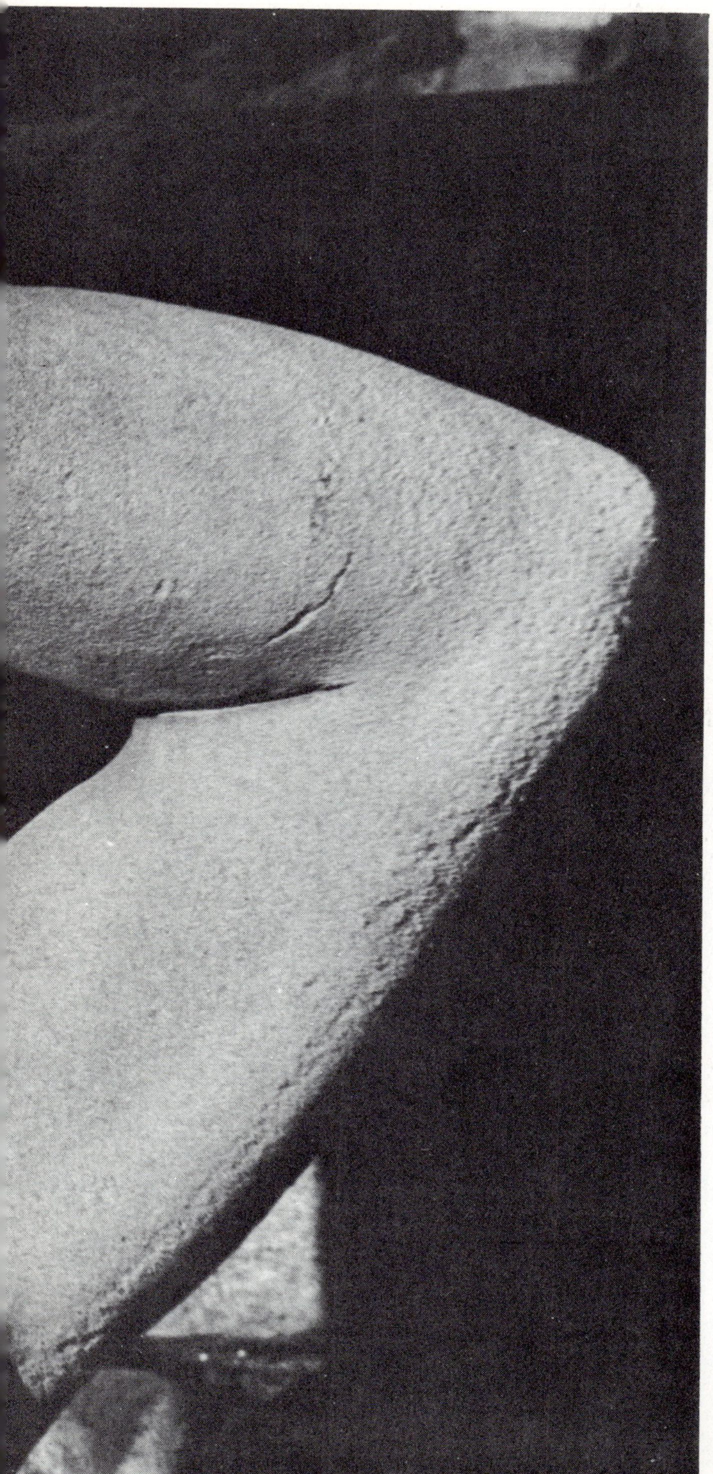

Some subjects cannot be composed by rearranging them or seeking a different shooting angle. The sculpture at left is part of the relief work on the base of a fountain. Unable to shoot in any way other than square-on, the photographer composed his subject within the edges of his frame to create a strong considered composition. Photo by Rafael Fraguada.

FRAMING

Just as the frame surrounding that painting on your wall sets it off from the rest of the room, so the technique of framing sets the point of interest in your photograph off from all that surrounds it. In this respect the technique of framing can be one of your most creative tools in photography, and can turn an ordinary photo situation into a very exciting picture.

Let's take the picture of the old gentleman sitting on the park bench. We would usually see this kind of subject treated as a straight-on picture of a man reading his paper, shot from a standing position. That would be all; nothing to warrant looking at for very long, and certainly not very exciting. But the photographer took this ordinary subject and made it most interesting by using the device of framing. He crouched down at the end of the bench and shot through the metal braces, framing his subject's face.

There are many natural frames which can be used effectively to create a more interesting picture—trees, windows, fences, etc. They help to give a feeling of unity to the picture, and, if the framing device is nearer to the camera than to the subject, it will give a feeling of depth to the photograph. Framing also tends to "pull" the viewer into the picture.

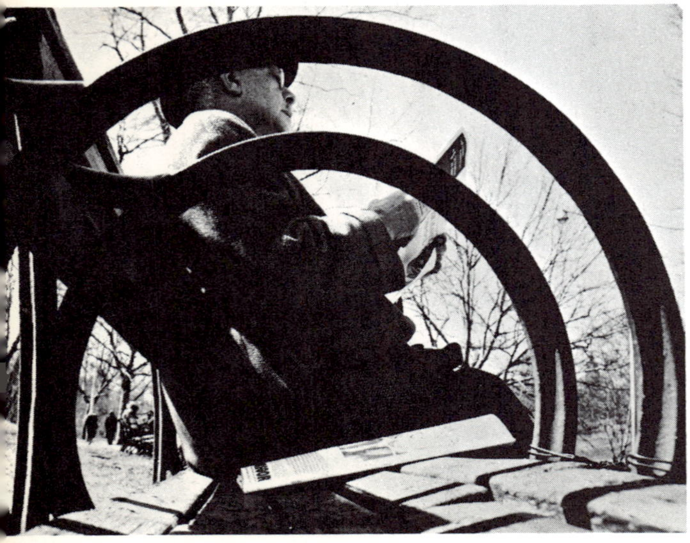

A strong "framing" element within a photo can be used to direct the eye of the viewer. Attention is directed in the photo at the left to the subject's face. In the photo at right, the entire subject is framed within the doorframe in a fence along a New York pier. As the subject was strongly backlit by the setting sun, the fence acted as a sunshade and provided some interesting texture around the subject rather than the detailless overexposed background that would have been recorded had the subject and photographer stepped beyond the fence. Photo at left by Horst Schafer. Photo at right by Patricia Maye.

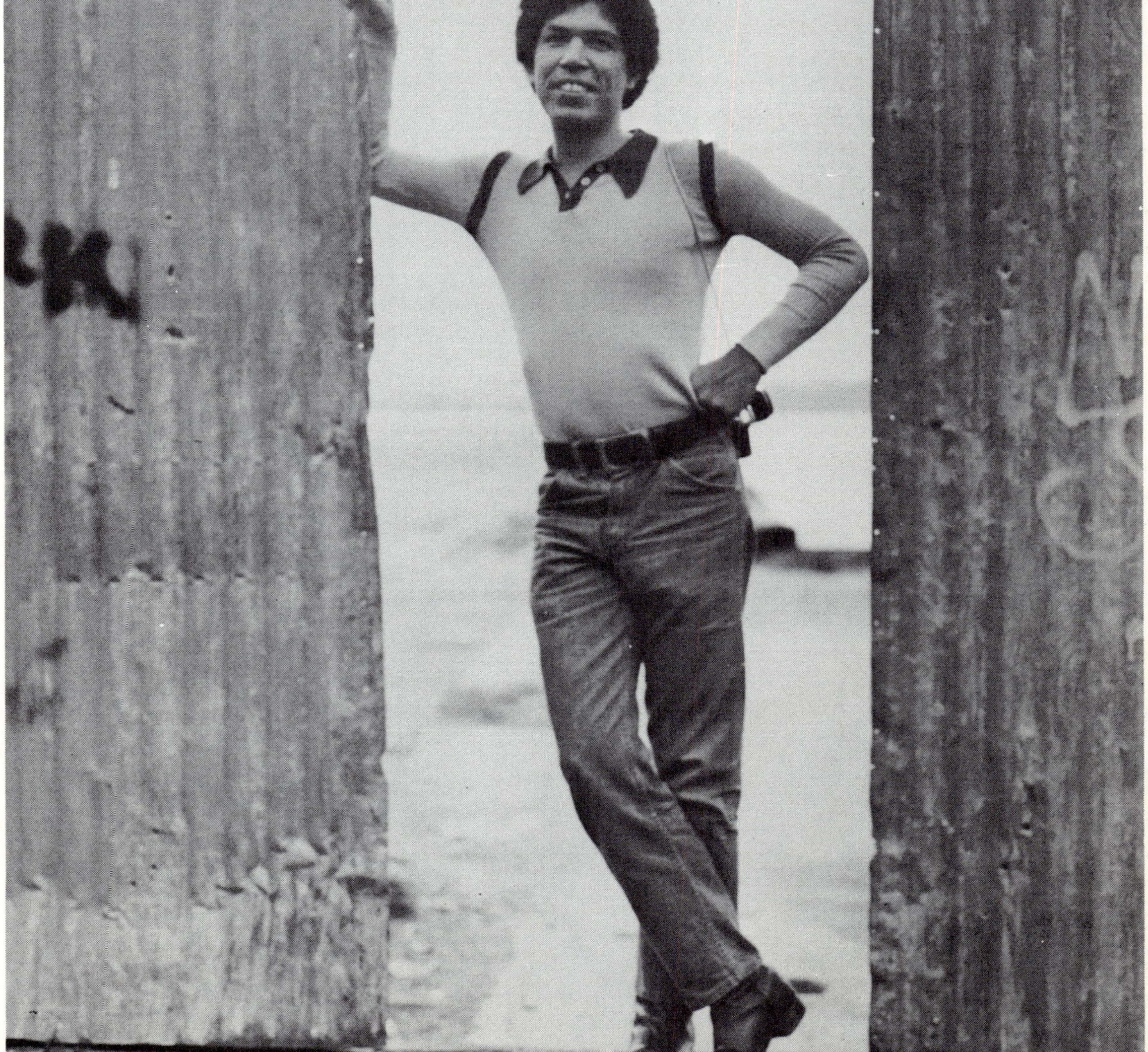

SIMPLICITY

Some of the most exciting pictures you'll ever take will be composed from one small detail rather than a whole conglomeration of things. Pictures in which you try to include too much will end up busy, overpowering and confusing. But if you can train yourself to eliminate all the extraneous matter that conflicts and detracts from the message you are trying to tell, you will find that you have created a thing of beauty, the detail of which will tell more eloquently what you were trying to express than the "whole" ever could.

The picture of the young boy (below) was taken in a very beautiful English-style courtyard. It was the photographer's original intent to capture the boy within these surroundings. On looking closer she noticed the intensity of the boy's eyes and saw that *they* were the focal point. So, instead of following her original purpose, she placed the boy in front of a contrasting textured background which would add interest but not distract from the boy's eyes. The simplicity of the setting makes a strong picture. The inclusion of the unusual buildings would have relegated the boy's intense expression to the sub-dominant position.

Carrying simplicity a step further, photographer Rafael Fraquada found and photographed the handsome pattern of light, shade and geometric forms in a city doorway (page 68).

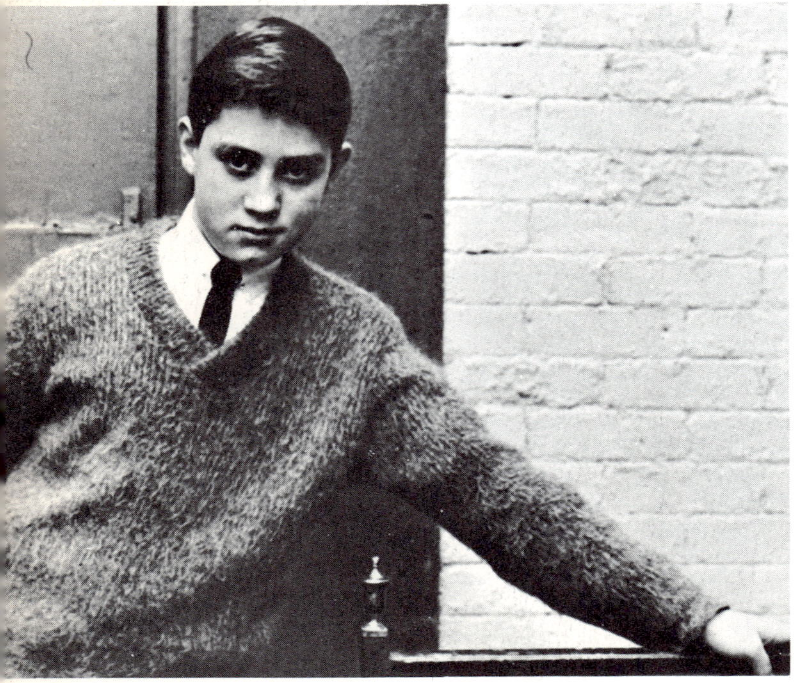

Simplicity requires the deliberate elimination of all extraneous elements from the photo. The close cropping of the portrait at left was done in the camera. The photo of the cat at right was cropped in the printing. Too much space was included above the subject in shooting so the necessary adjustment was made after the fact. Photo at left by Kathy Wersen. Photo at right by Patricia Maye.

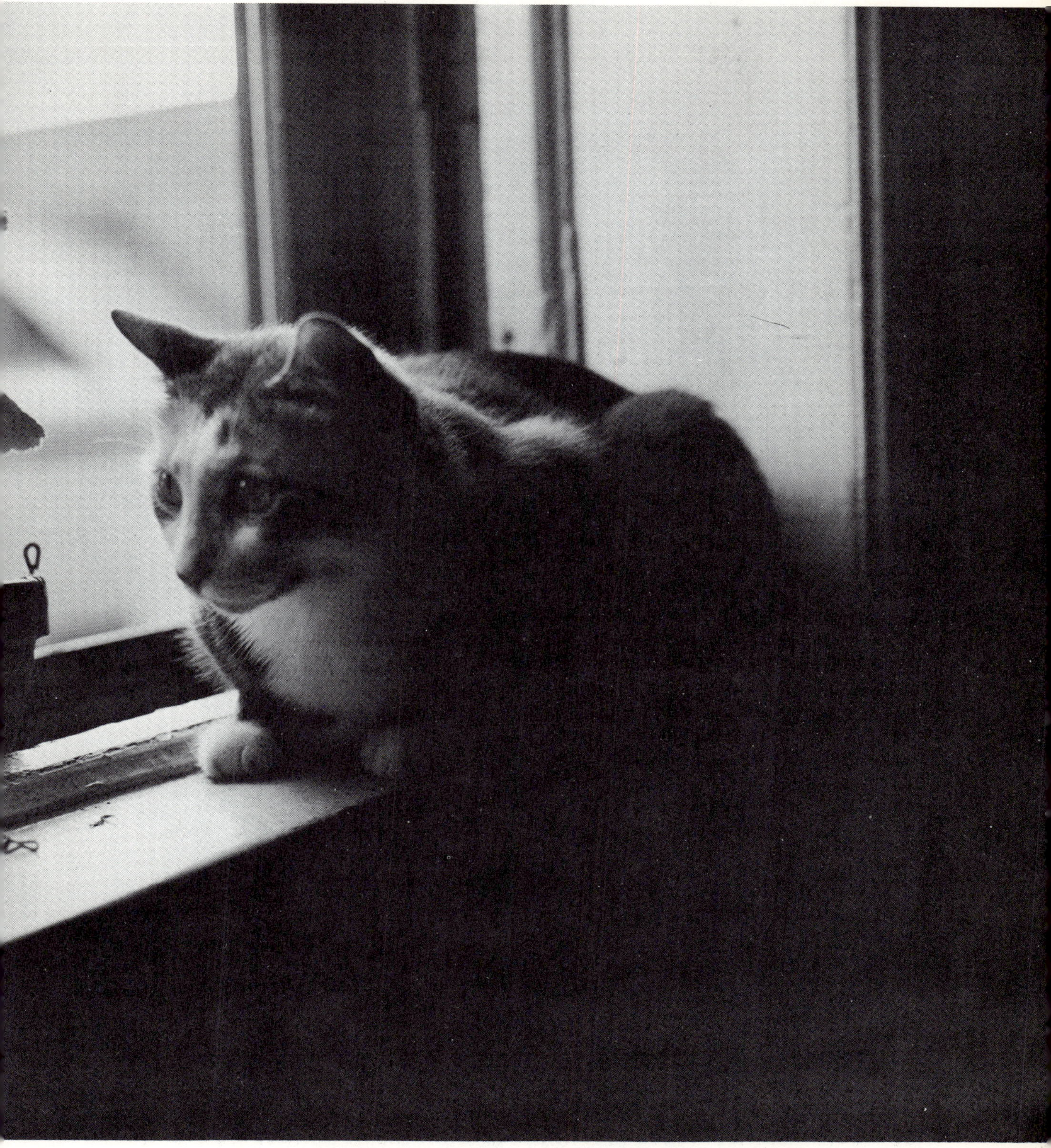

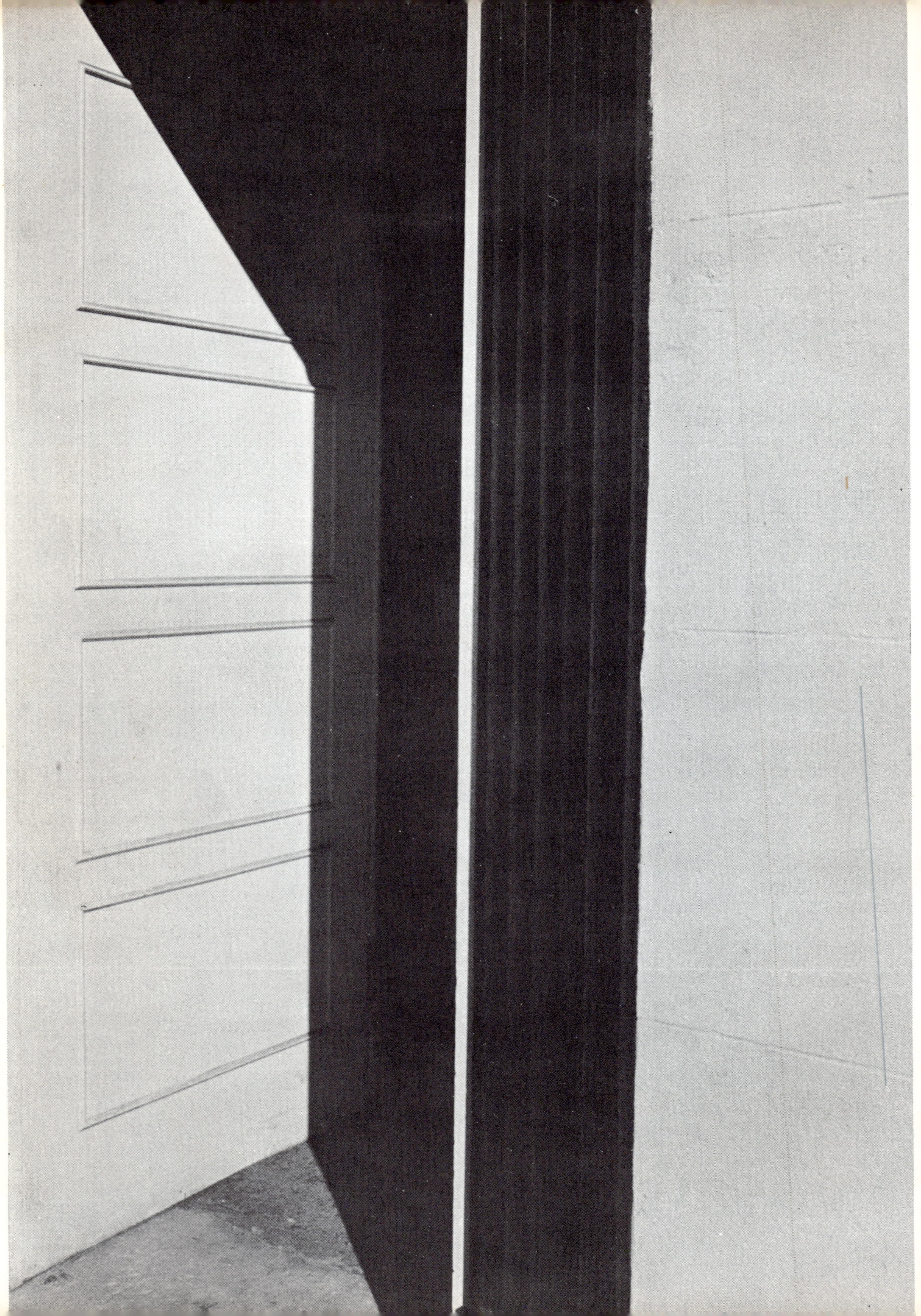

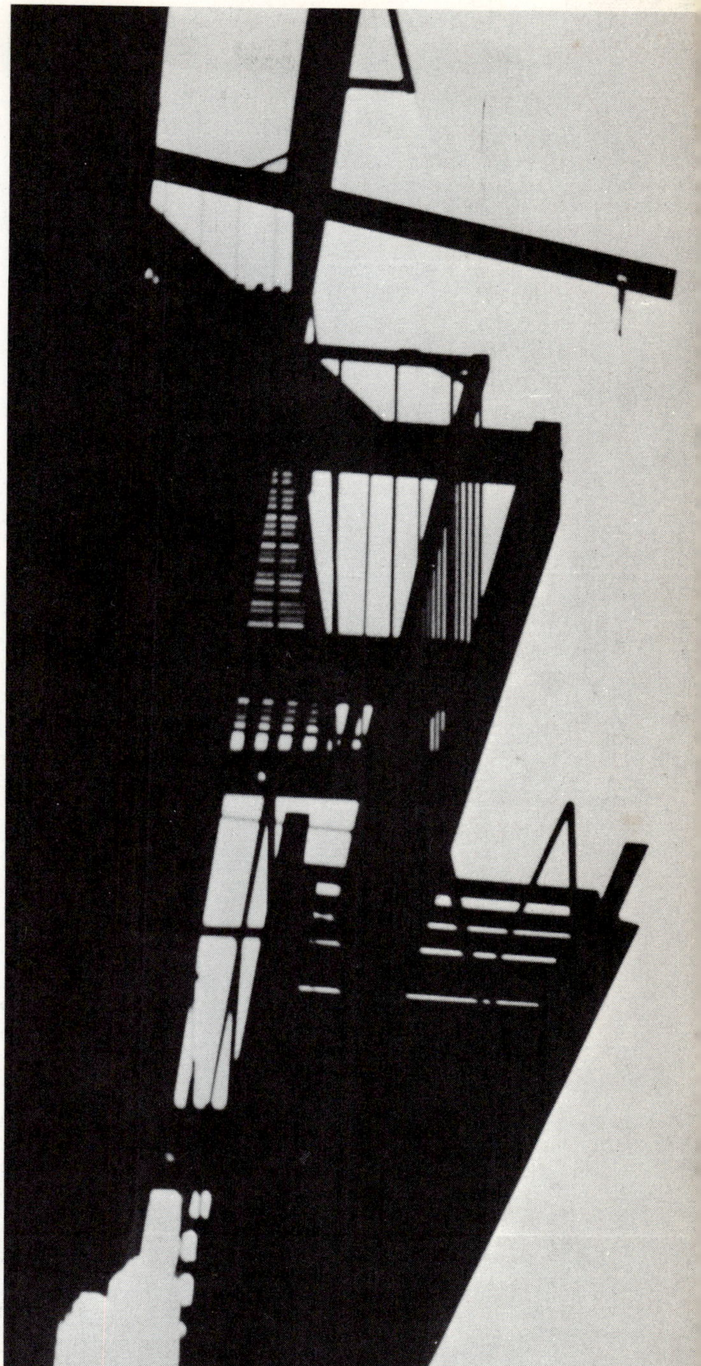

The two photos on these pages are essentially pure design. The highlights and shadows of the doorway opposite caught the photographer's eye as he was walking along one bright afternoon. The fire escape at right was photographed against the light to deliberately create a high contrast result. Photo at left by Rafael Fraguada. Photo at right by Patricia Maye.

PERSPECTIVE

You've probably seen professional photographers hanging out of trees, lying on their bellies holding up traffic, or in some of the hundreds of unnatural positions they seem to twist into. They aren't doing this to be amusing—it's an intricate part of their job. They're searching for the best angle of view from which to shoot their subject.

Most professionals stalk their subjects. They move in close, then back up. They walk all around the subject, check angles from above and below—and sometimes even from behind. There's a usual angle of view for most subjects—the professional is searching for the *unusual.* With a wide variety of shots to choose from, the final selection is then made in the darkroom.

The perspective of a picture refers to the choice of position from which the picture is made, or the angle of view. Sometimes the perspective is determined by what you want (or don't want) in the background. Sometimes it is chosen to "flatter" your subject. For example, if the subject has wrinkles or an unattractive neckline it is better to shoot down. Sometimes it is chosen to reveal the subject's point of view, as in photographing children at their level. Too often the adult tends to shoot down at the child; these pictures can be made more exciting when shot from the child's eye-level or by getting lower and shooting up.

A strong case is generally made for the "naturalistic" rendition of subjects—especially in portraits. And, children are supposed to be photographed at their own eye level to avoid results exactly like that at the right. But, never ignore the temptation to break the rules and take a picture with a novel viewpoint. The photo at right was taken as the photographer strolled along with the subject, her nephew. She aimed down at him with a 35mm lens and photographed him just as he was—striding along, smiling, and bedeviling her with an endless series of questions. Photo by Patricia Maye.

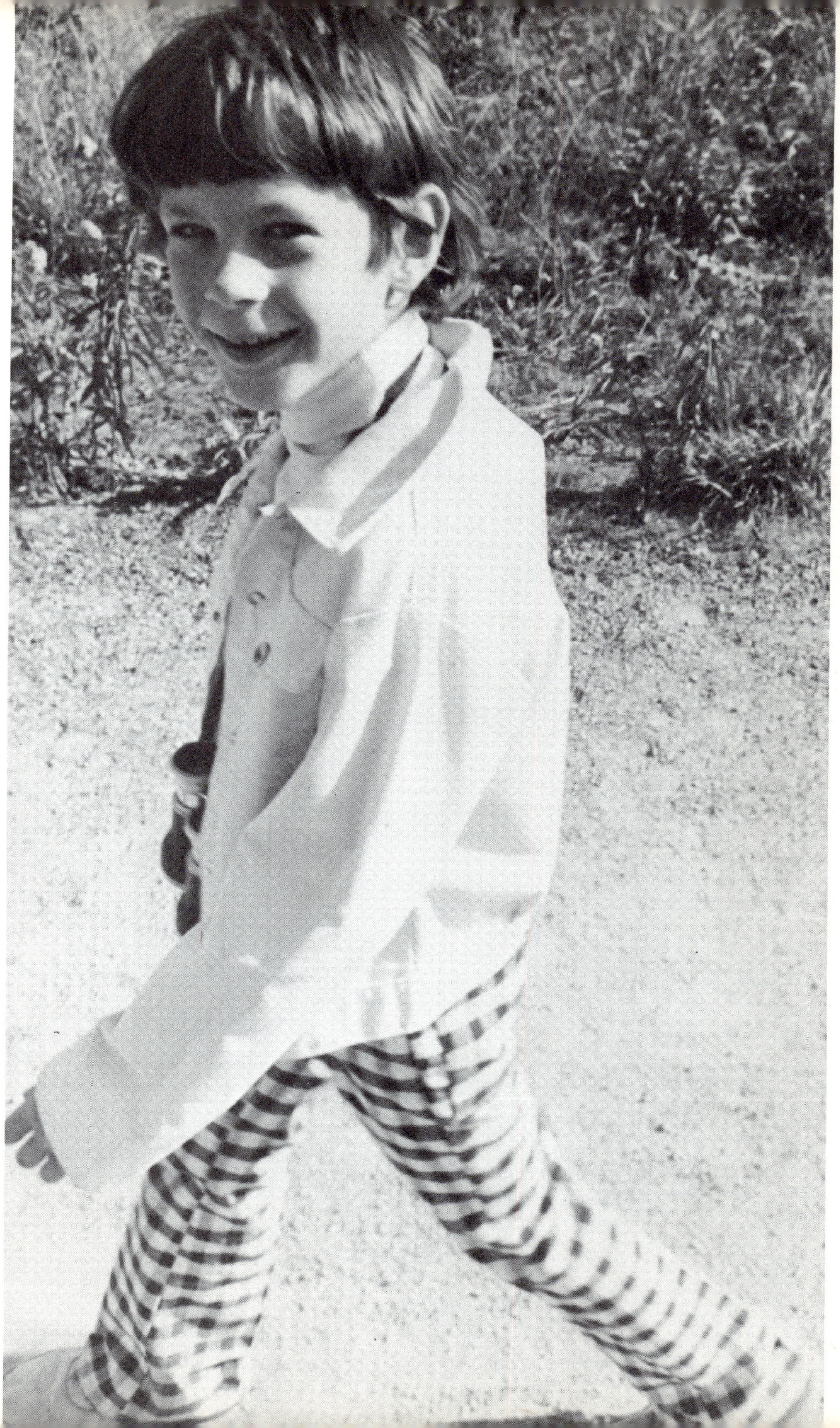

ISOLATED MOMENT

In most situations there is a tiny, subtle moment during which the whole meaning of the situation is summed up. This is what Cartier-Bresson has called the "decisive moment." We call it the isolated moment because it is such a fleeting thing that once gone can never be recaptured, at least in exactly the same fashion. It is as though for a second in time everything hangs suspended, giving meaning and purpose to life, and then the world goes back on its merry, chaotic way. Gone, but not lost, if you have been clever enough to capture it with your camera. In order to record these moments you must train yourself to be on the lookout for "little" things. If you can anticipate and select them, you will get them.

The picture (below) was taken on a bus. The old lady got on, sat down, gazed out the window, then suddenly noticed the little boy next to her just as he turned to look at her. For a fleeting second they regarded each other companionably, then turned back to their own thoughts and the moment was gone.

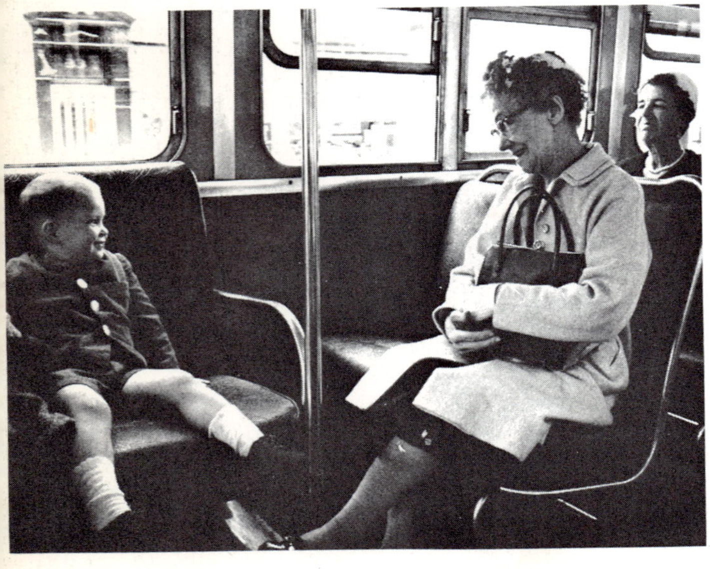

Contemporary photography is truly an instantaneous medium and, in the midst of the general hub-bub of things, it falls to the perceptive photographer to recognize and record instants of interest and meaning. As described in the text above, the photo at left was taken on a bus and successfully recorded the moment of recognition between two passengers. The candid photo at right was taken at a family get-together as a lovely lady shared an intimate word and gesture with her grandson. Photo at left by Kathy Wersen. Photo at right by Seymour D. Uslan.

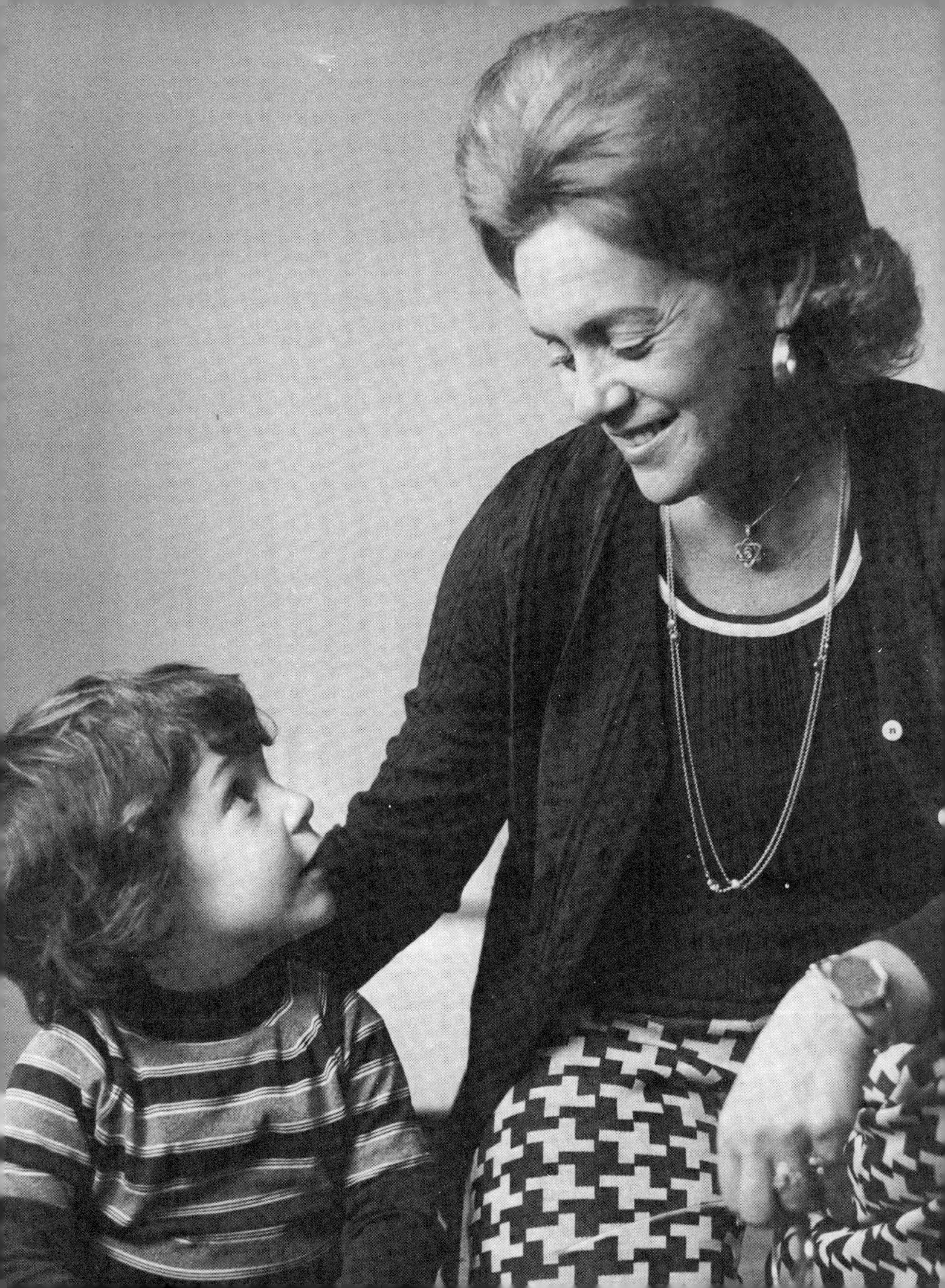

HIGHLIGHTS AND HIGH CONTRAST

The photograph below is a startling one. The eye is immediately drawn to the brightness of the Chinese boy's face, lighted by the sunlight reflecting through the glass door. Such a bright spot in a photograph is called a highlight. Sometimes these highlights are quite subtle and not so noticeable. Many times they can be used to express something which the photographer fleetingly sees and wants to record. In this case it was the abstract quality of the highlight in the boy's face, giving it the appearance of an oriental ceremonial mask.

In order to have an effective highlight area in a picture there must be sufficient contrast between the highlight area and shadows, either because of differences in tone or of lighting. Strong, contrasty sidelight will create good strong shadows and emphasize surface texture. Once you've found a subject, take an exposure reading and then underexpose about two stops; to achieve dark, contrasty shadows.

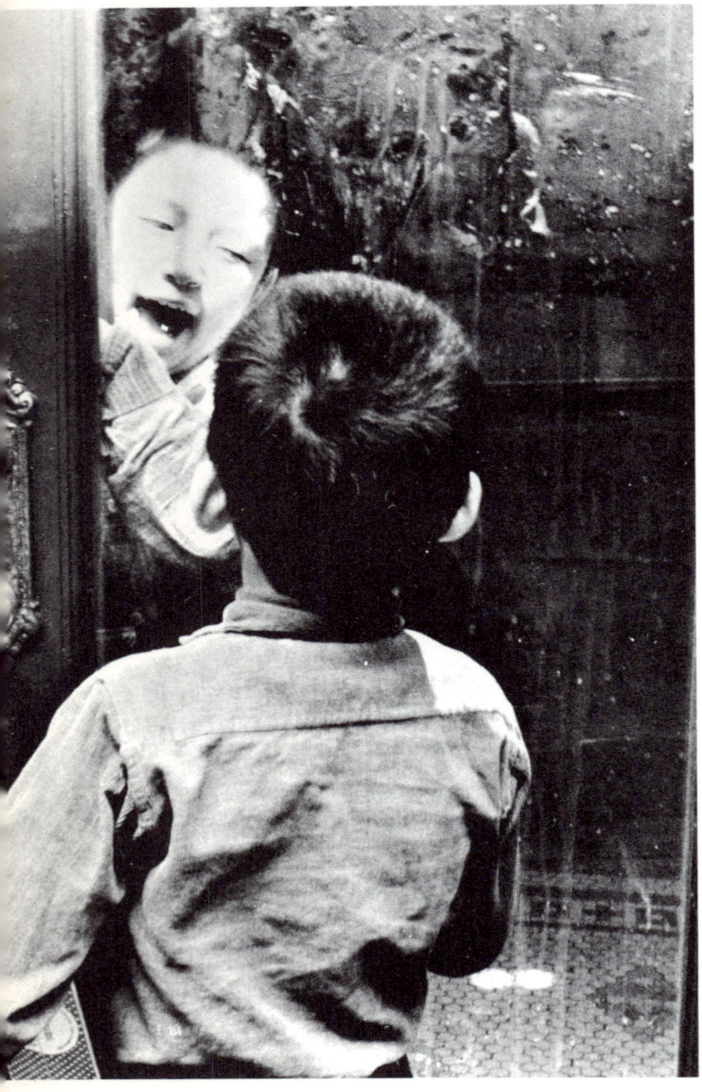

Learning to read the world in tones of black and white is a hard first step for the beginning photographer. But, some experimentation with lighting and exposure coupled with a new skill at seeing subjects in terms of light and dark, highlight and shadow, will soon lead to expressive photographs. Highlight areas such as the boy's face in the shot at left demand the eye's attention. Dark shapes on a light background such as those in the two photos at right give a feeling of drama. Photo at left by Horst Schafer.

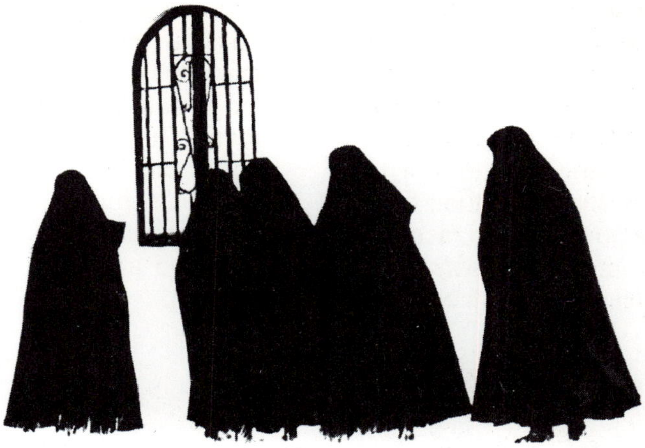

This high contrast print is the result of some tonal manipulation after the fact. The original negative was printed on high contrast paper and certain extraneous elements were painted out with white. Then the retouched print was rephotographed on high contrast film and reprinted on high contrast paper. All gray tones were eliminated in the process. Photo by Horst Schafer.

This high contrast print was made directly. The birds and lightpole were recorded as silhouettes as they were photographed against a bright sky background. The negative was printed on high contrast enlarging paper to strengthen the effect. Photo by Horst Schafer.

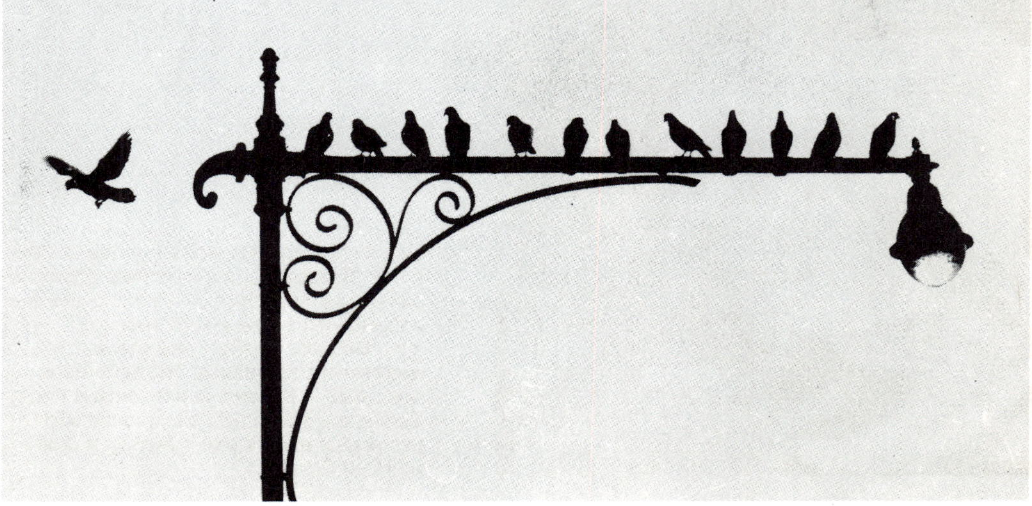

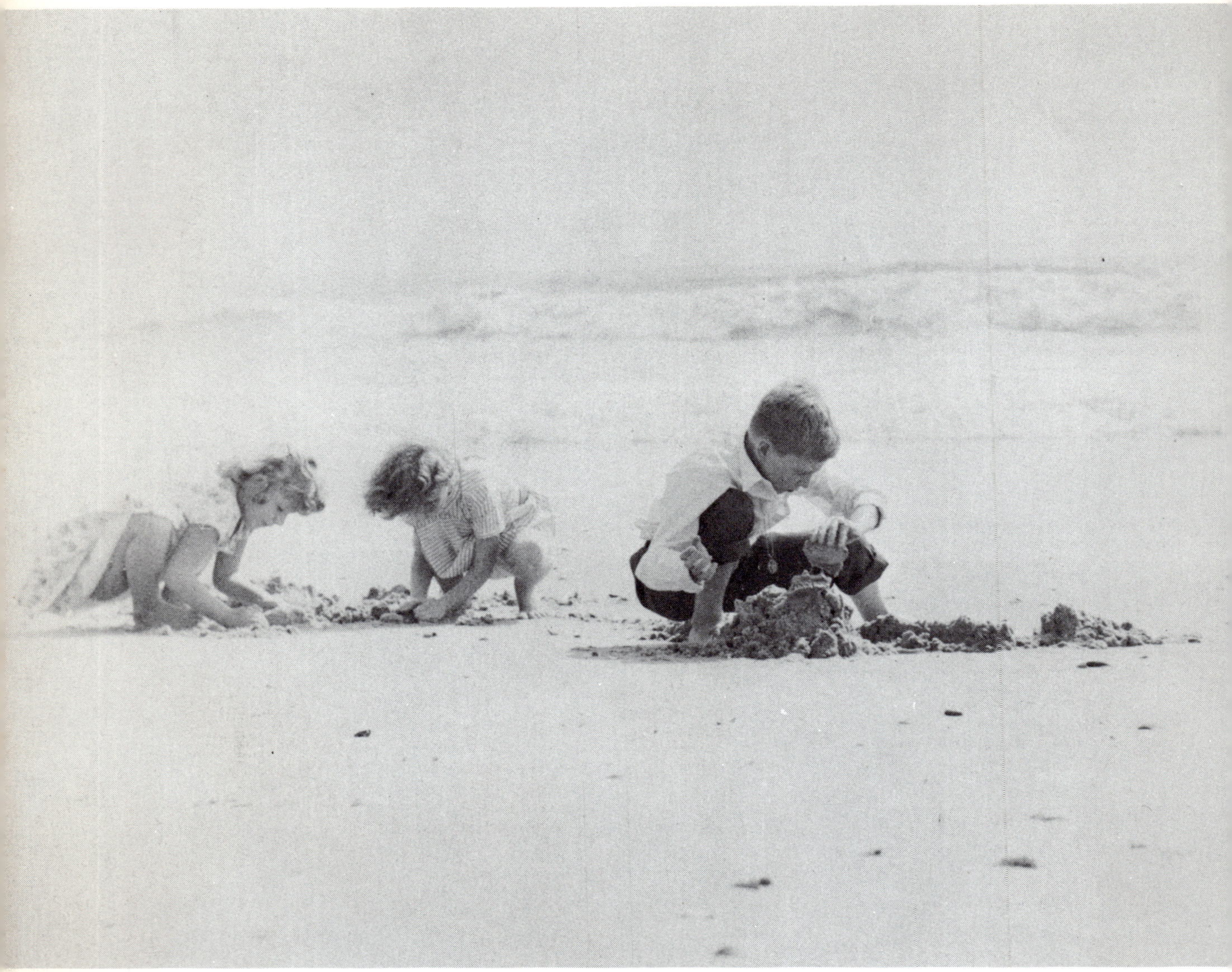

The photos above and at right were printed on high-contrast paper to eliminate middle tones. Photos by Patricia Maye.

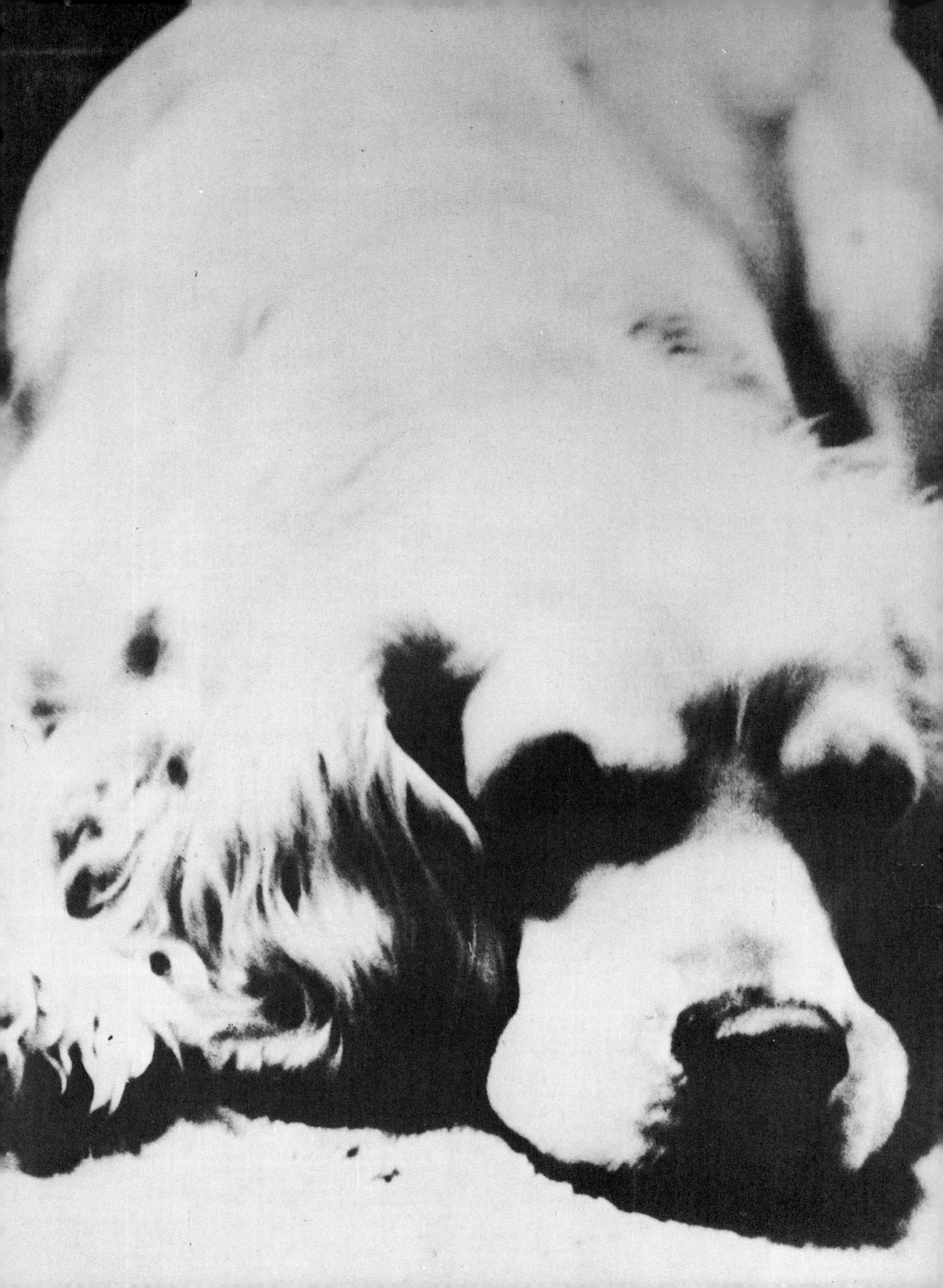

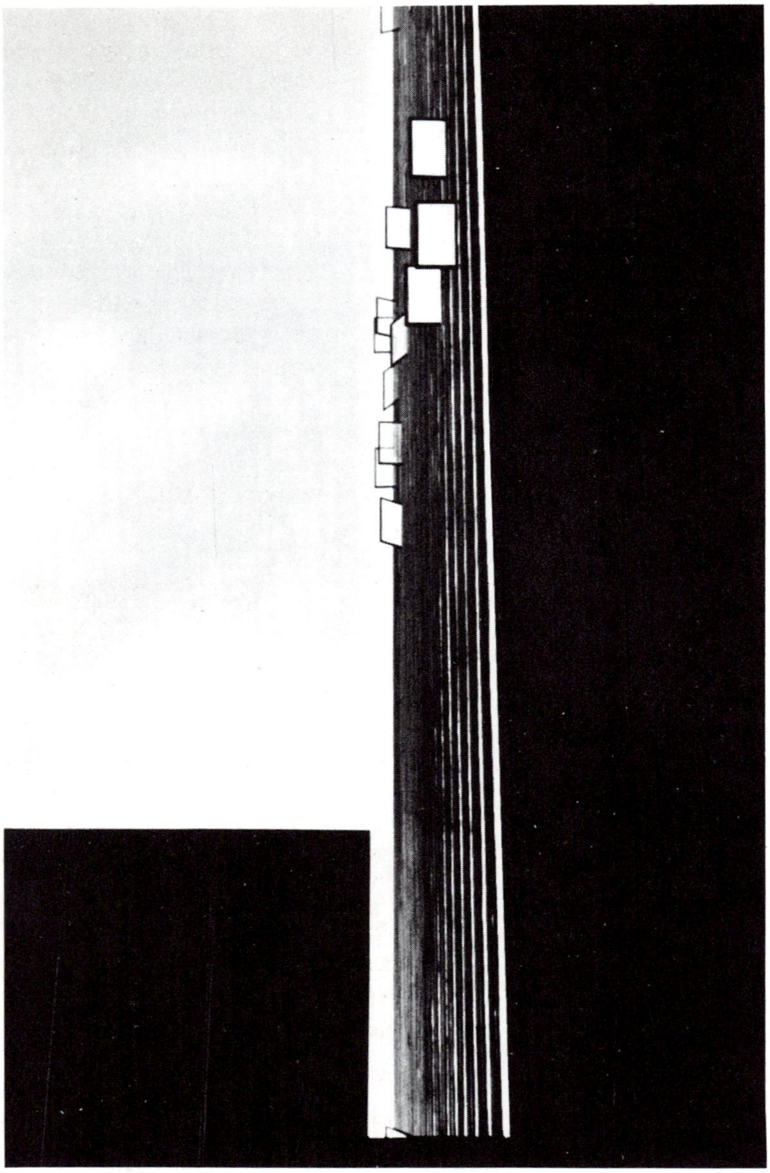

The symmetry of this highly designed photo is broken only by the irregular shapes of the open windows. Rather than destroying the total effect, the window lends a vitality of the otherwise formal arrangement. Photo by Horst Schafer.

AN EYE FOR DESIGN

Design is everywhere around us—but it takes an awareness that it exists in order to see it. If you do not have this awareness built in, you can train your eye to see it. All it takes is a little experience and the knowledge of what to look for.

Certain subjects lend themselves to pictures of design through their vertical and horizontal lines. For example, in the picture on page 75, the pigeons could have been shot with more of the city behind and with more exposure given to the overall picture so that the shadow areas registered detail rather than black silhouette forms. Then we would have had a picture of pigeons on a pole as the eye sees it—but not a picture of strong design. By underexposing the pigeons you can still recognize them from their shapes, and we get a simple design effect similar to Mondrian's in the artist's world.

Sometimes a picture suggesting strong design is first seen in the camera's eye, at other times we don't see it until we look at the contact sheet; this is especially true in black-and-white photography. Strong designs can be made from normal negatives by making a contrasty internegative on photolith high contrast copy film to eliminate the middle tones, and then making a very contrasty print.

The buildings in the picture on page 78 and the palm leaves, below, are examples of overexposure so that the black areas would go dark, creating the design effect.

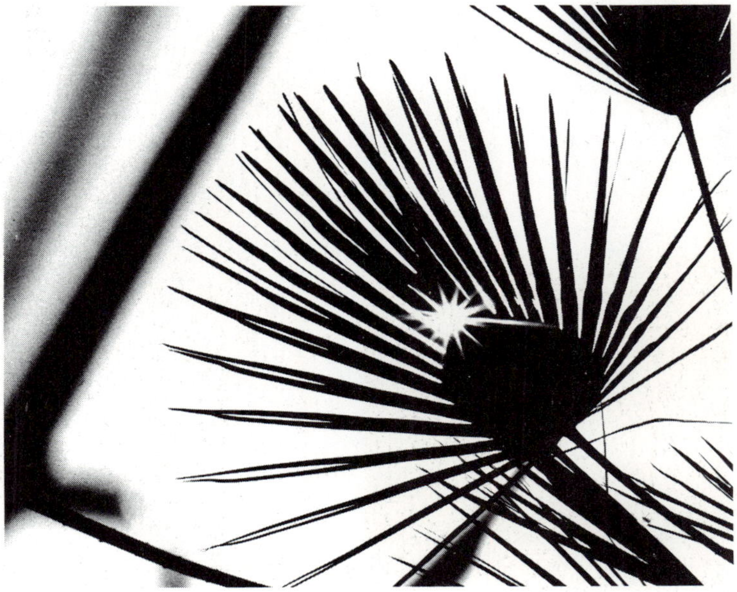

The natural pattern of a strongly backlit plant was the raw material for the strong design above. The star shape is the sun, refracted as it passed through a narrow opening in the plant. Photo by Horst Schafer.

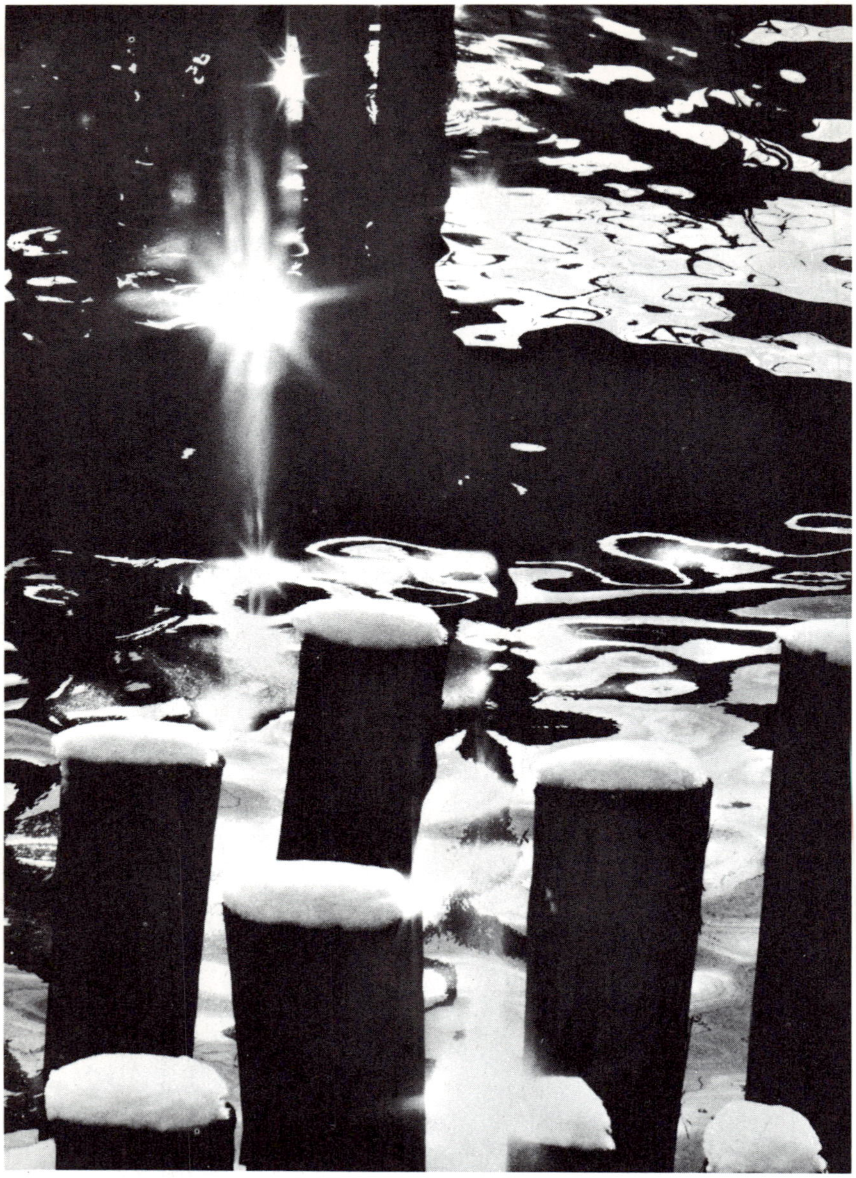

As the photographer's eye for design becomes more finely attuned to the world around him, seemingly uninteresting subjects can become the source of handsome photographs. The snow-topped pilings above might not even catch the attention of an unattentive viewer, but they provided one photographer with a handsome, mood shot. Snow is also a contribution factor in the delicate photo at right. The fine pattern of the twigs against the fresh, new-fallen snow is both source and subject of the composition. Photo above by Horst Schafer. Photo at right by Rafael Fraguada.

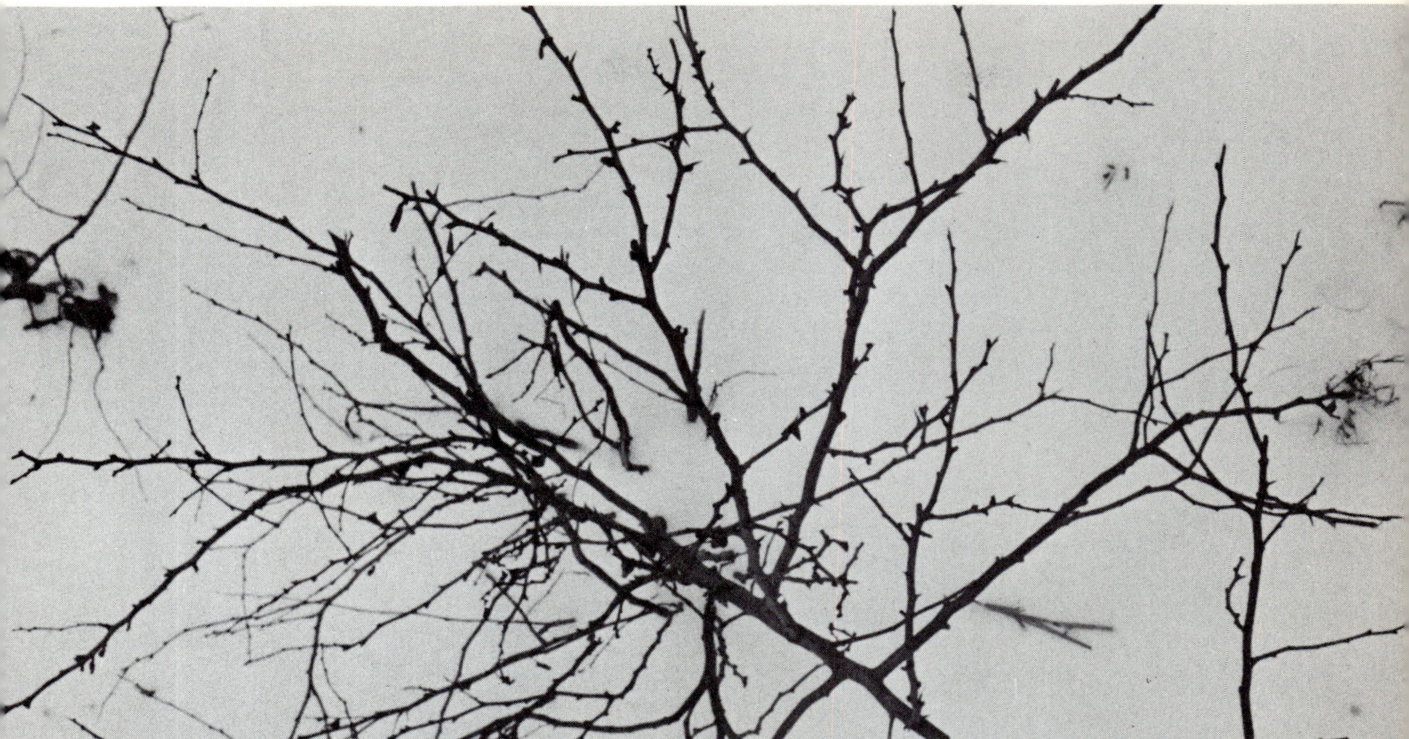

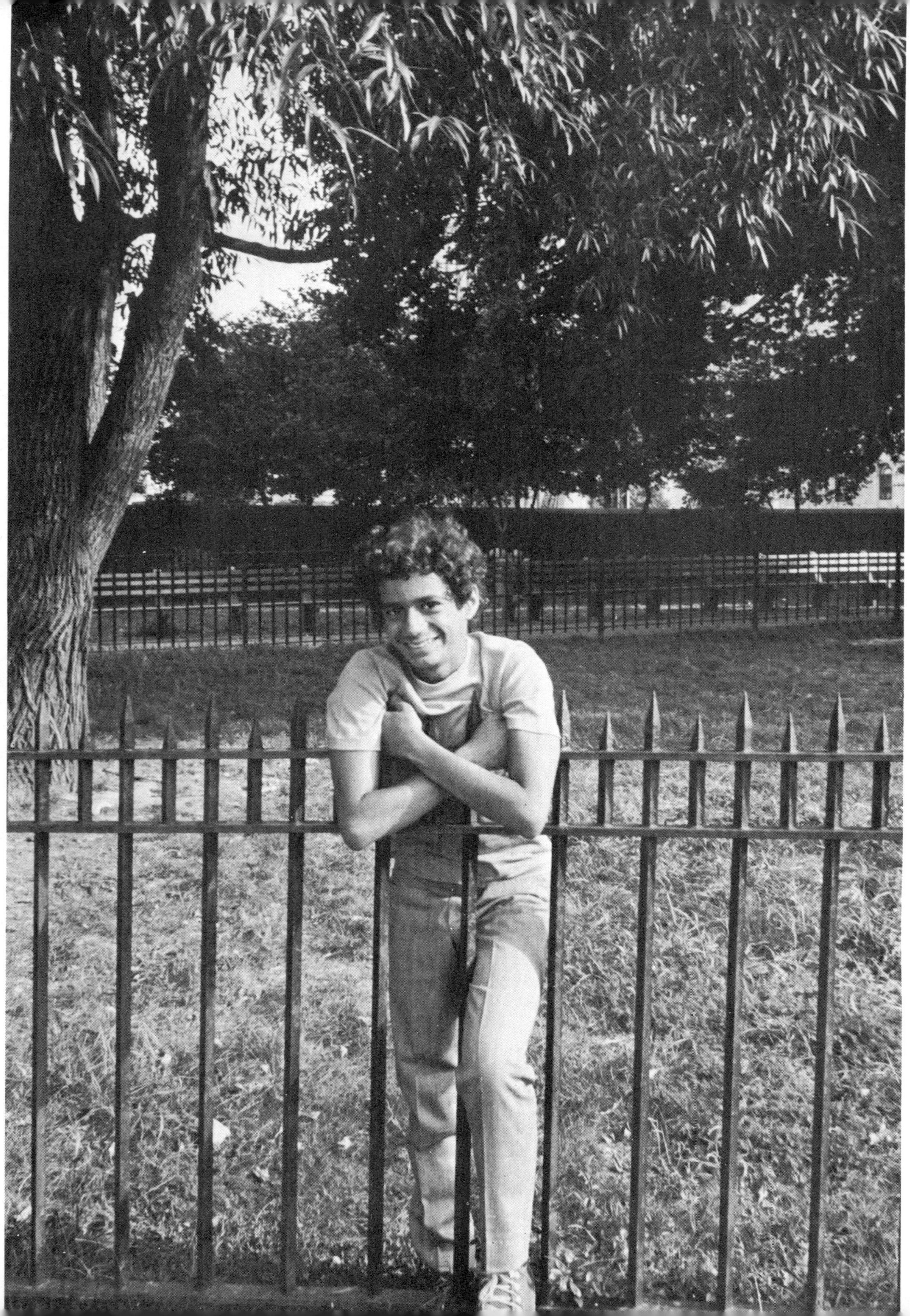

5

POPULAR SUBJECTS

Portraiture is a favorite persuit of almost all photographers. The smiling subject at left was photographed during an afternoon shooting session in and around New York's Central Park. A few words of conversation established a rapport between the photographer and subject and won the winning smile which would have been impossible in a "sneak" shot. A 35mm lens used at a reasonable distance from the subject took in a good portion of the shooting locale. Photo by Rafael Fraguada.

PORTRAITS

An imaginative portrait does not have to be made in a lavish professional studio—it can be made at almost any time, any place and under any condition—if you put your imagination to work. A good portrait not only reflects the subject's likeness, but his personality as well. It tells something about him as a person; and often the non-professional has a better chance of capturing that special quality in a friend or family member than a professional studio photographer has. With a 35mm camera you can take a variety of shots quickly and capture many moods and expressions. And because of the camera's unobtrusiveness, it is easier to capture the "unfrozen" moment, particularly if you engage your subject in something of interest to him.

The portrait on page 85 was taken in the subject's office. He felt comfortable because "business was going on as usual." This happy moment was caught during an engrossing conversation with one of his clients. He had forgotten all about the camera. In the picture of the family group, the photographer wanted something a bit different than the usual stiffly posed shot showing four generations. He involved the adults in a game with the child, climbed up on a ladder and shot down. The result—a relaxed picture with a creative twist.

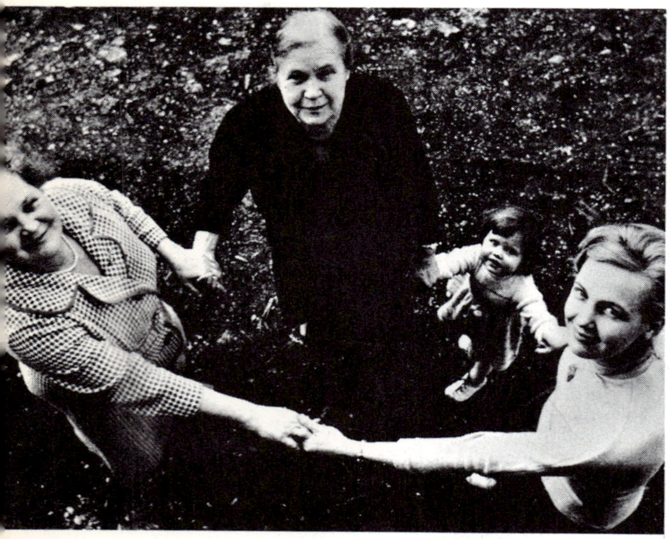

A bird's-eye view was used to photograph four generations of one family in the photo at left. The head shot at right was photographed from slightly below the subject's eye level. It served as a jacket photo for the subject's book. An air of naturalness was maintained by photographing the subject in his office. Photo at left by Horst Schafer. Photo at right by Kathy Wersen.

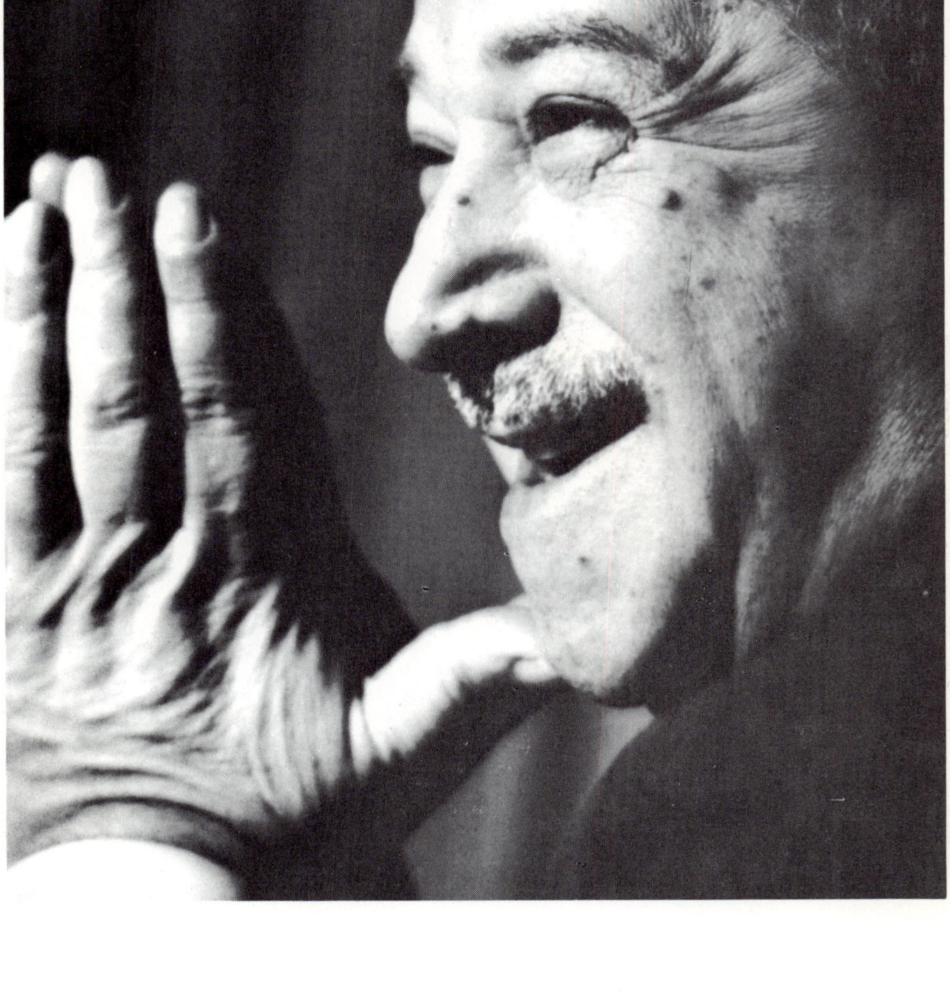

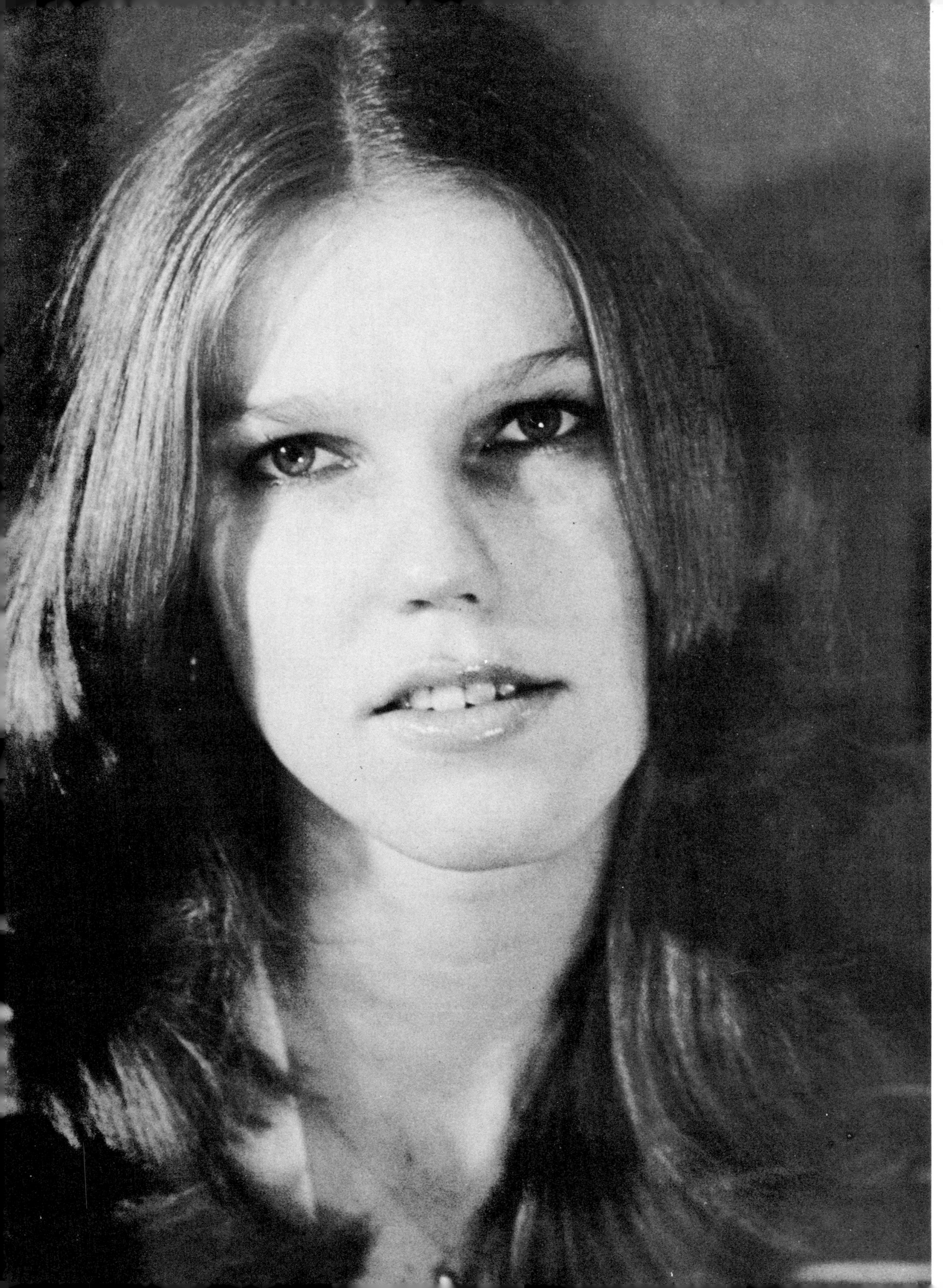

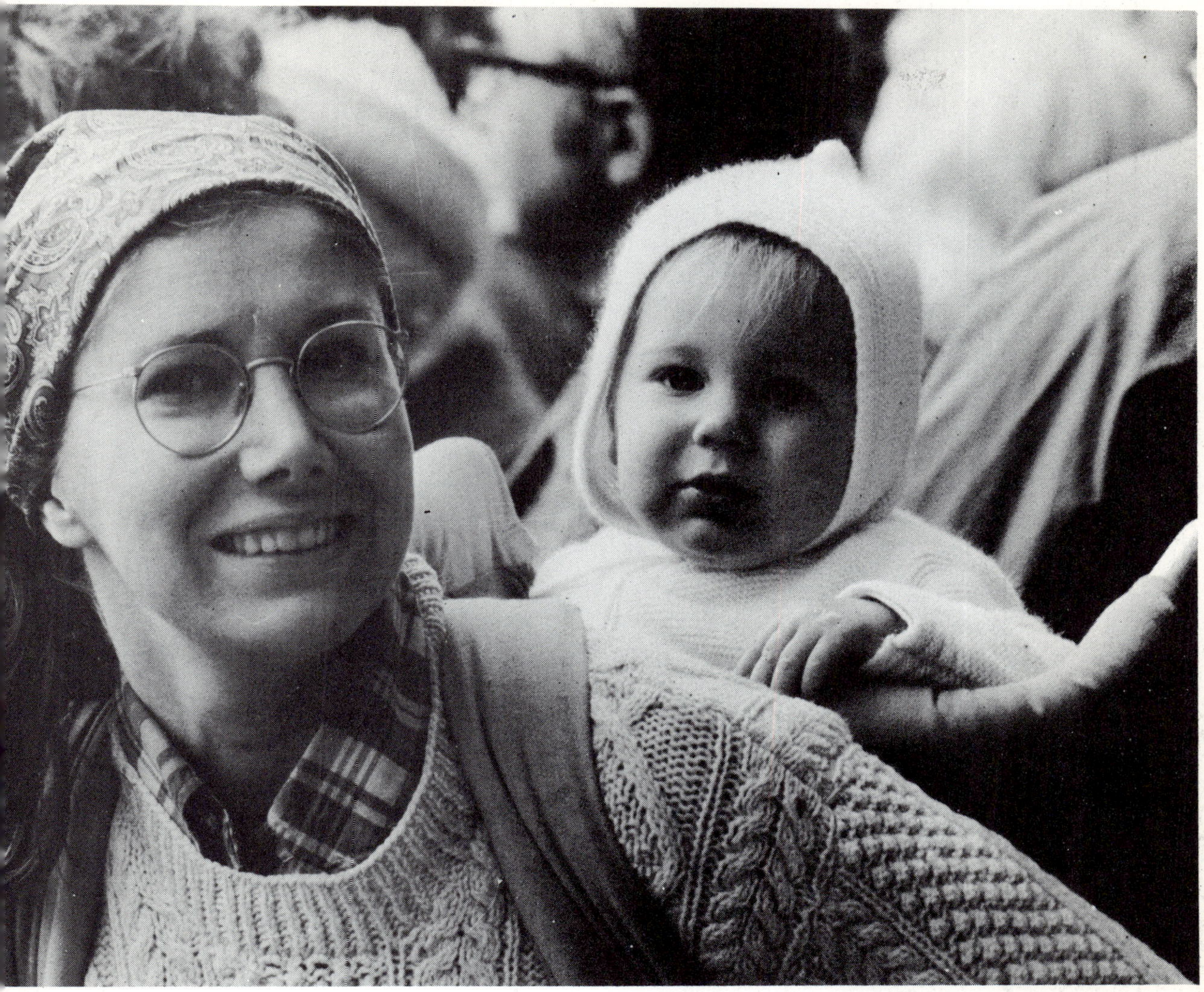

Both the photos on these pages were taken with longer-than-normal lenses. By using the Soligor 75-260mm zoom lens and shooting from across the room, the photographer was able to achieve the tight head shot opposite without crowding the model. The double portrait of the mother and child above was taken from about ten to fifteen feet away with a 200mm lens. Photo at left by Patricia Maye. Photo above by John C. Wolf.

CHILDREN

When you choose babies and children for your photographic subjects you simply cannot miss. There is no such thing as an ugly child. But! Your creative ability can enhance even the loveliest child. First, forget all the stuffy poses you have ever seen children subjected to. Let them breathe—move about. If you must work in a confined area, give the youngster something to play with or to do. Soon he'll forget about the camera and you'll get the opposite of those "smile for the birdie" type pictures.

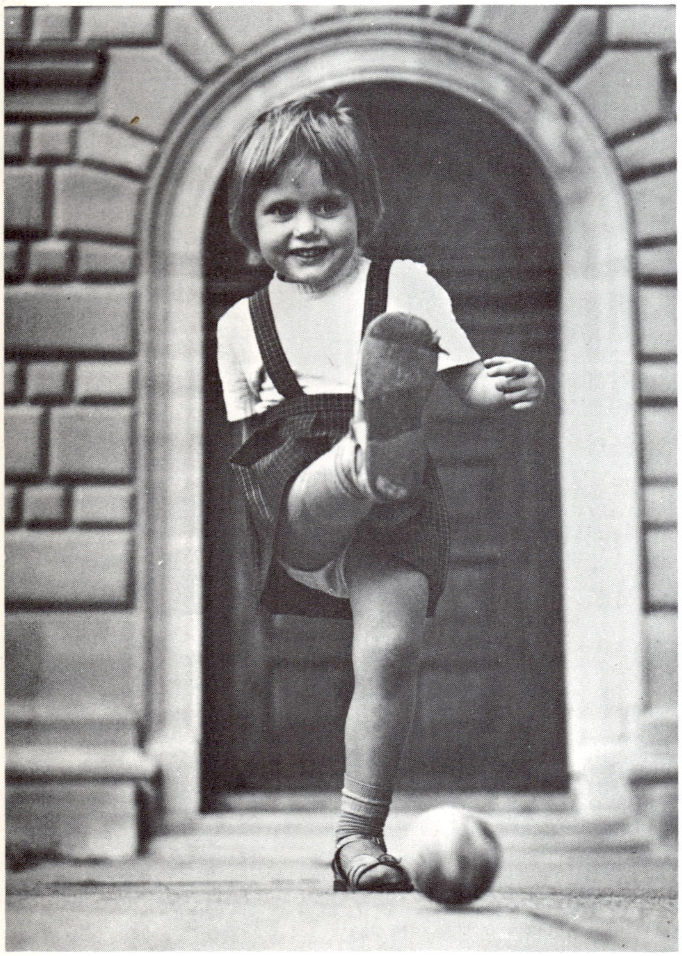

Photographing children requires both patience and imagination on the part of the photographer. Two primary rules should be taken to heart. The first is to try to understand what the child would like to do. The second is to absolutely forget all the standard poses unless and until the child falls into them naturally. The photo at left owes its vitality to the low viewpoint and the natural activity of the child. The photo at right is also shot from a non-standard viewpoint but this time not by the photographer's choice—the subject had taken to a tree. Photo left by Horst Schafer. Photo at right by Roy F. Sullivan.

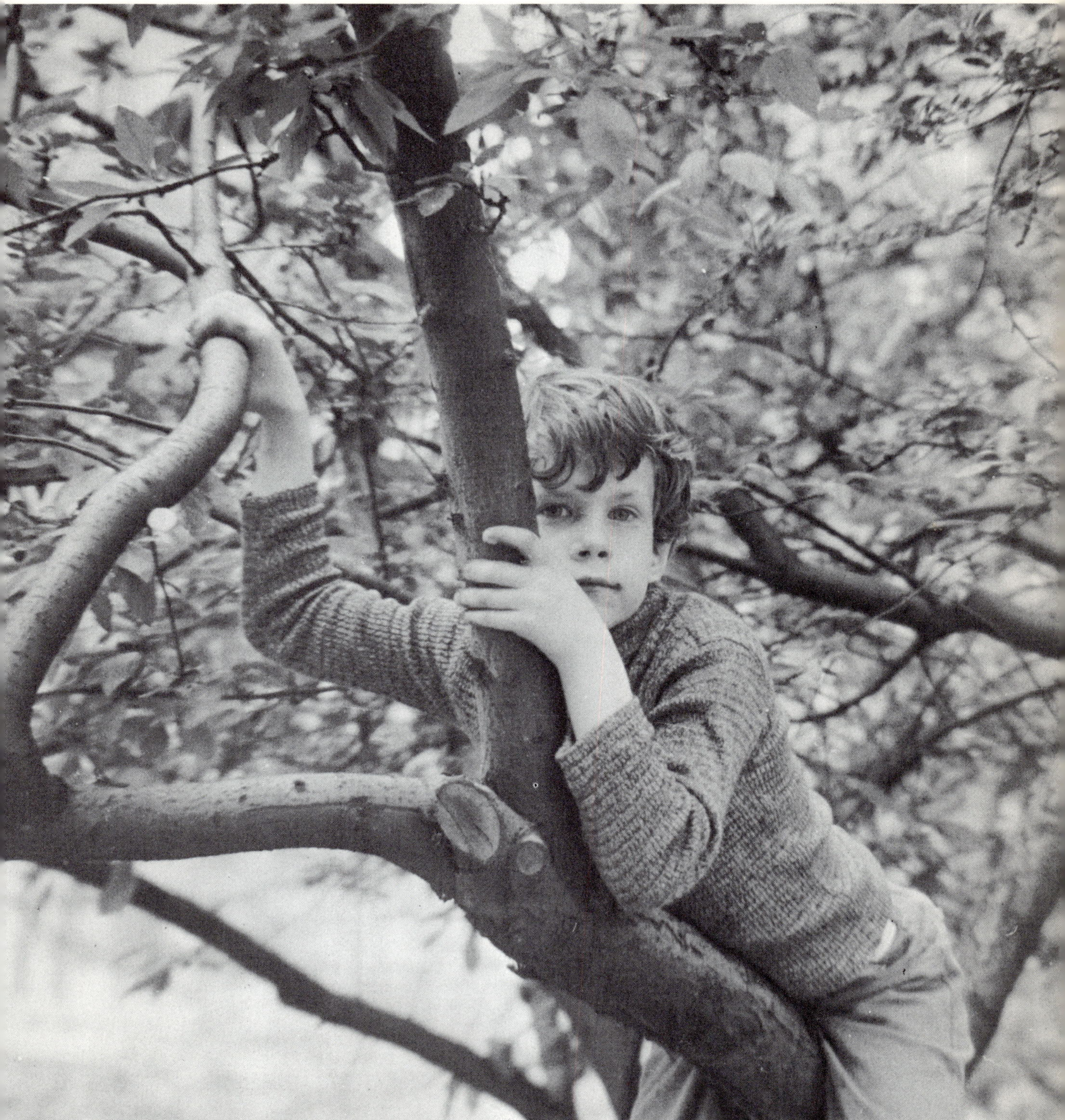

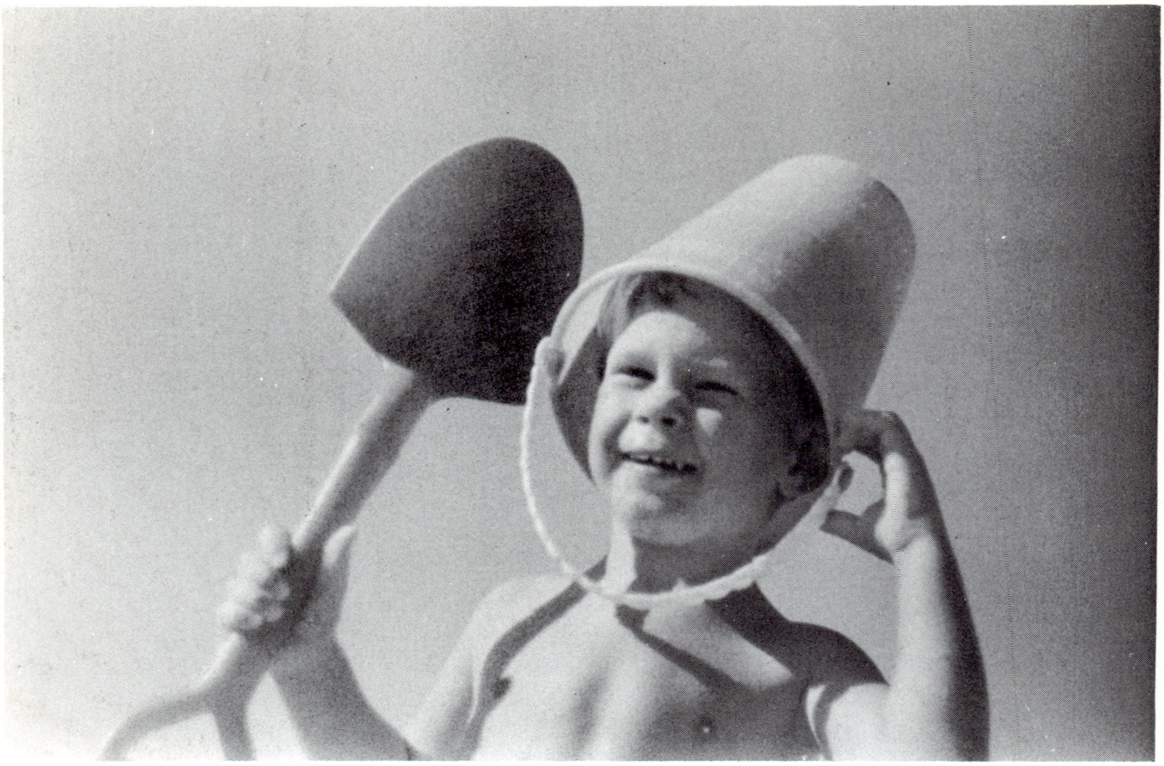

Occassionally the photographer is blessed with a child subject who would prefer nothing more than to have his picture taken. This was the case in the photo above. Assuming that sufficient shots had been taken, the photographer began a conversation with the little boy's mother. Unwilling to give up the spotlight, the subject materialized with his beach pail on his head and inquired—"You like me party hat?" Needless to say, the shooting session was resumed. The subject at right was very busy with his roller skates and completely indifferent to the photographer. He neither participated nor resisted.

Both the children on these pages were put at their ease by a simple prop. Balloons, balls, musical instruments, and all manner of toys and tricks are useful accessories to the child photographer. Photos by Patricia Maye.

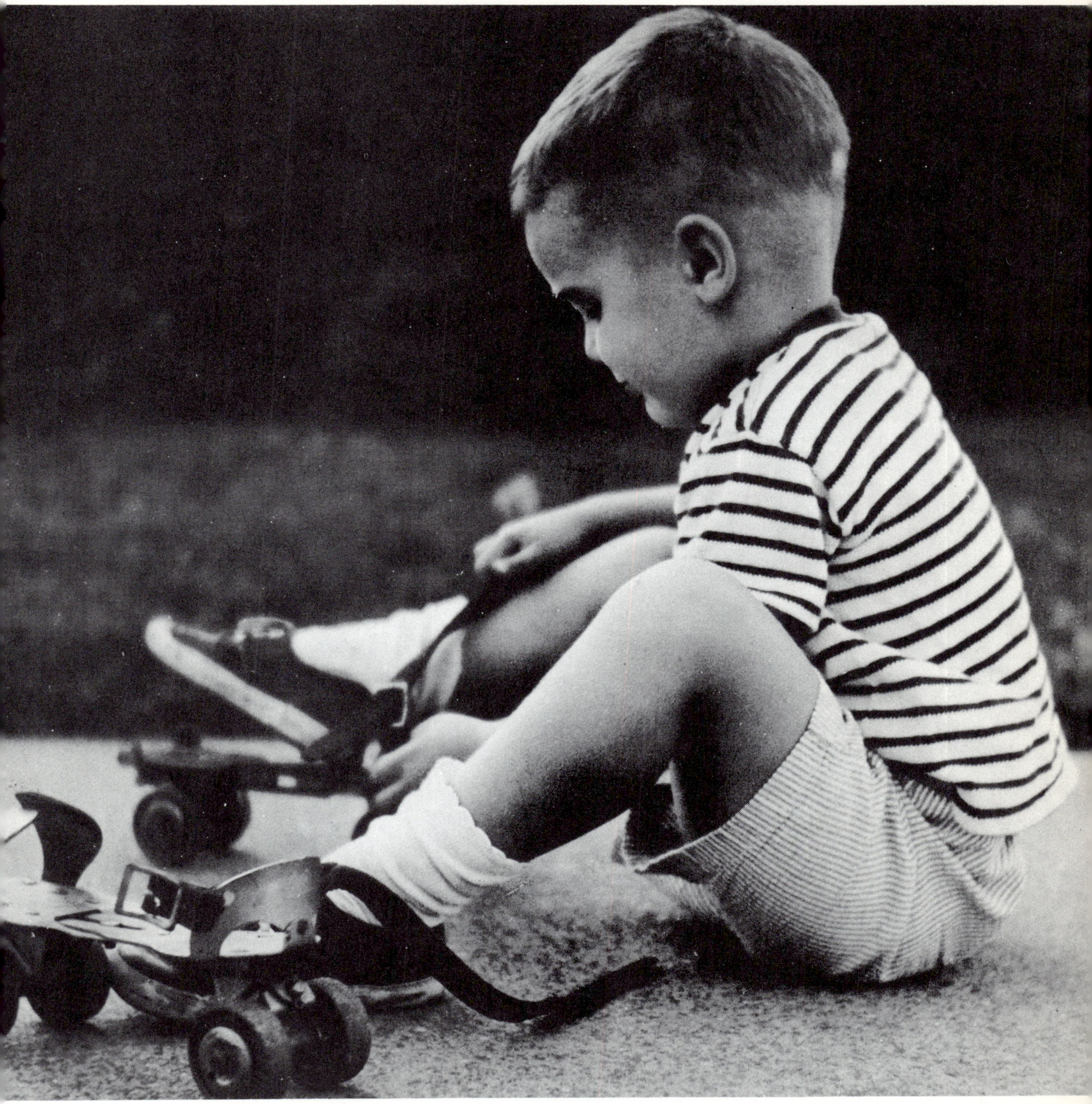

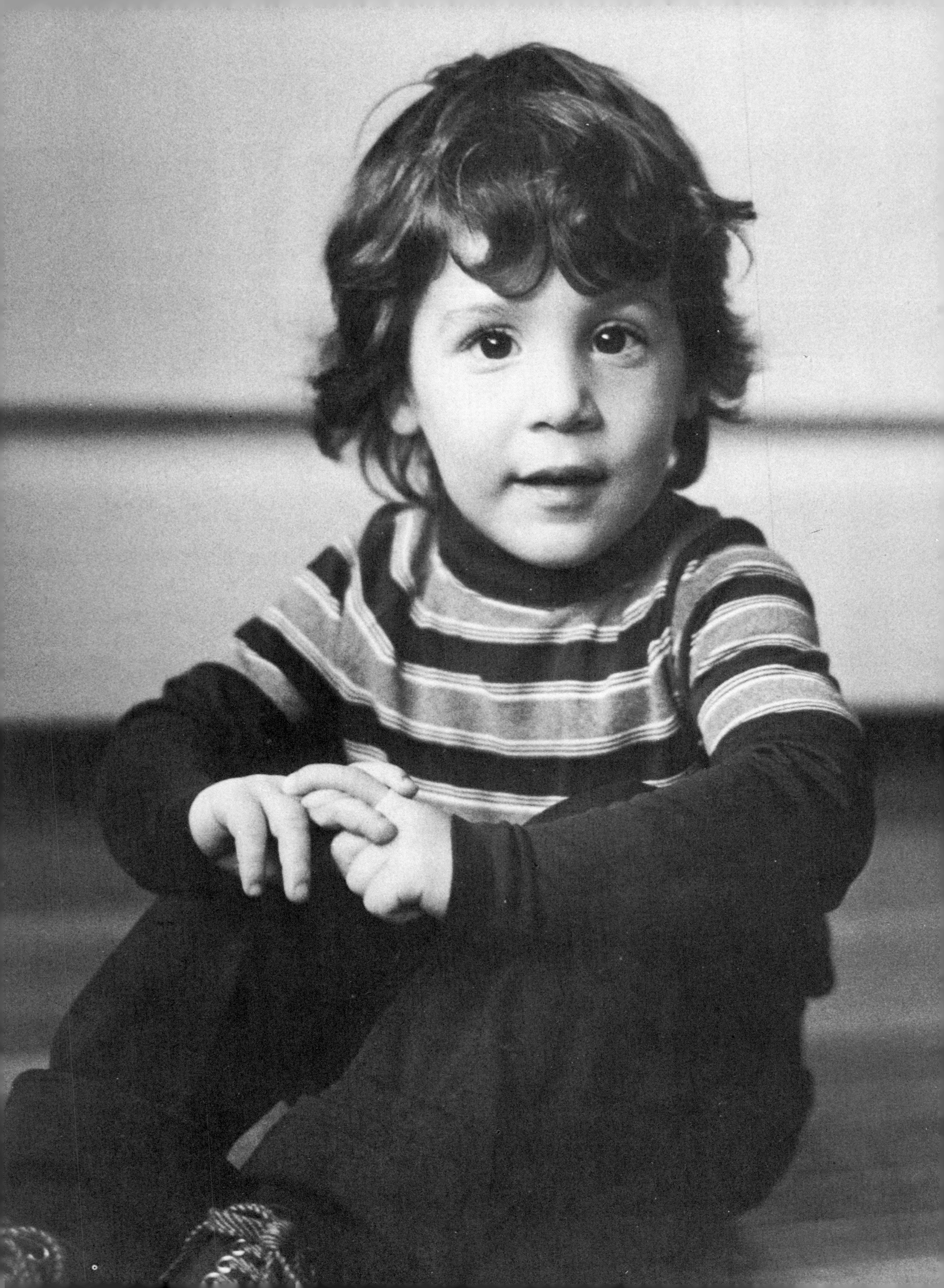

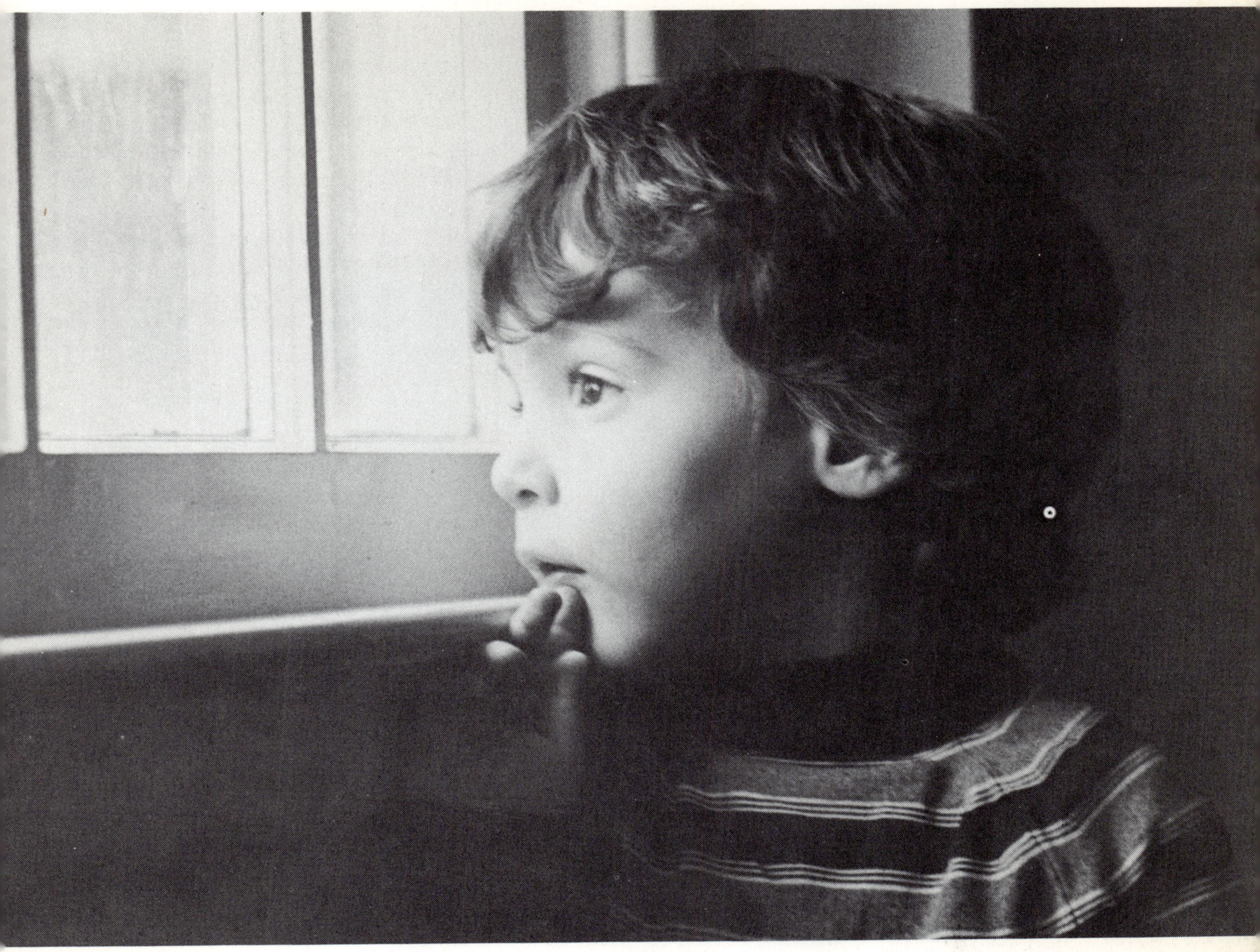

The two portraits on these pages were made by the subject's grandfather. Thus, a natural rapport existed beforehand between subject and photographer. The portrait at left gains strength from the direct eye contact from model to viewer. For the profile study above the subject was asked to look out the window. Despite the fact that the shot was posed, awkwardness was avoided because the little boy was not asked to do anything out of the ordinary and there was plenty to distract him outside the window. Both photos were taken on Panatomic-X film by available light. Keeping photographic apparatus to a minimum goes a long way toward achieving successful results when photographing children. Photos by Seymour D. Uslan.

ANIMALS

Animal pictures are almost inevitably destined for sure-fire success—even though animals can sometimes be more difficult subjects to photograph than humans! Many words of advice have been written on the importance of "making friends" with your furry or scaly or leathery subject before you start to shoot. Animals are like people—they have their own preferences and they usually can size you up a lot faster than you can evaluate someone you've just met. Dog yummies and other tidbits have their place in establishing rapport, and one professional swears by liverwurst. But, most important, animals, like people, are flattered when someone takes an interest in *them*. A few moments spent playing with or cooing at your subject may well pay off in a prize shot.

Remember two things when photographing animals. An animal has a personality—why not show it? And, you are a creative individual. Why not show your personal point of view in your pictures?

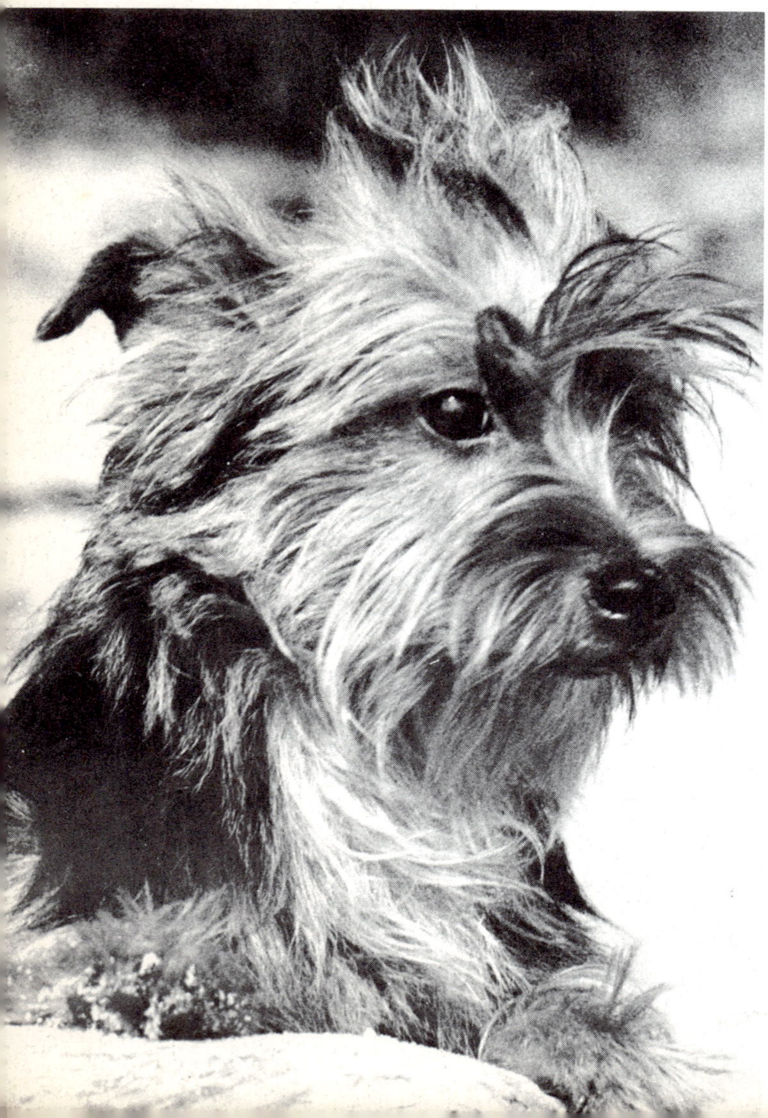

Pets are usually the first animals the beginner photographs. The secret is to show that something special that makes the subject special. The keen intelligent look of the little Yorkshire terrier at left caught the photographer's eye. And, believe it or not the Spaniel shown on page 49 was every bit as poetic as he seems in his portrait. The cat at right was deliberately photographed against a shadowy background with exposure calculated for her light spots. Her inquisitive look is eternal. Both the shots on these pages were taken with longer-than-normal lenses. Crowding an animal subject will put it at ill ease as easily as crowding a human subject will. Photo at left by Kathy Wersen. Photo at right by Patricia Maye.

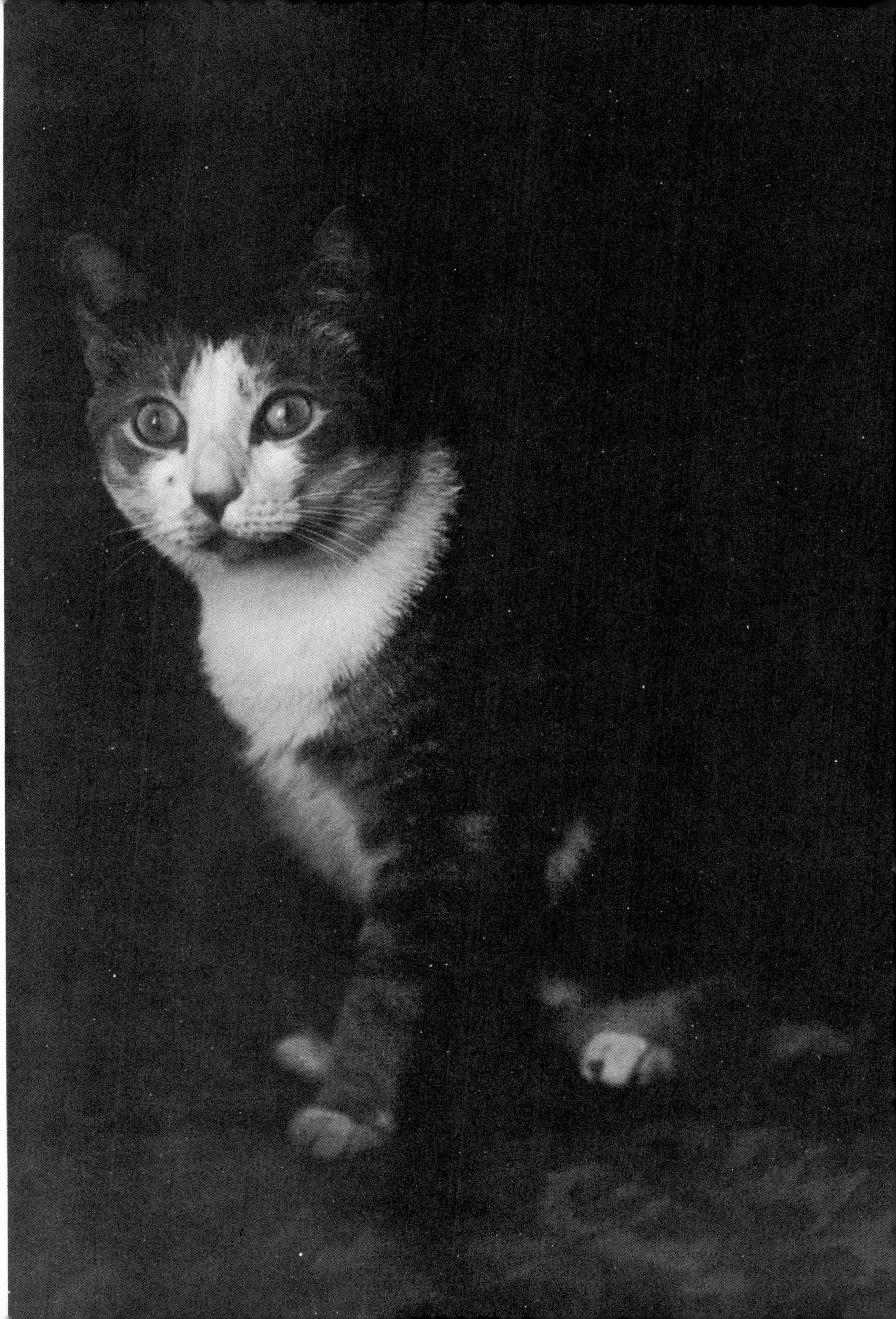

TRAVEL

Taking a trip is one of the most stimulating times in any photographer's life. With so many new and exciting things to see, there are pictures everywhere. You'll want to record them all so you can relive the fun over and over. But if a picture is worth more than a 1,000 words, then why not try for the unusual shot rather than the overworked type of mother and dad in front of the Washington Monument, squinting into the sun, in a "cheese" picture that says nothing? You know the type.

Here are a few hints. Don't wait till you arrive at your destination to start shooting. Keep your camera around your neck or someplace handy —not packed in the bottom of your suitcase. When you shoot landmarks, select the unusual angle or try to include people in action. Look for ways to frame the picture. Keep a keen eye out for the off-beat or unusual. Capture the local color—as the old fisherman standing next to his boat on the Island of Ischia, near Naples. Get a feeling of the people and places you visit. Meet them on their own ground, try to capture what is uniquely theirs—and you'll have some marvelous personal pictures to bring home as souvenirs instead of standard picture-postcard shots.

The travelling photographer must consider the full range of photo subjects. If he sticks to landmarks he will return home with a collection of photos that could have been achieved by an air-mail mail order to a foreign postcard outlet. People are the most interesting foreign subject that one meets while travelling. Often they are happy to pose for photographs. The old man at right was a willing model. The shot was taken with a normal lens at a routine exposure. It succeeded because it gives a sense of time, place, and circumstance. Photo by Kathy Wersen.

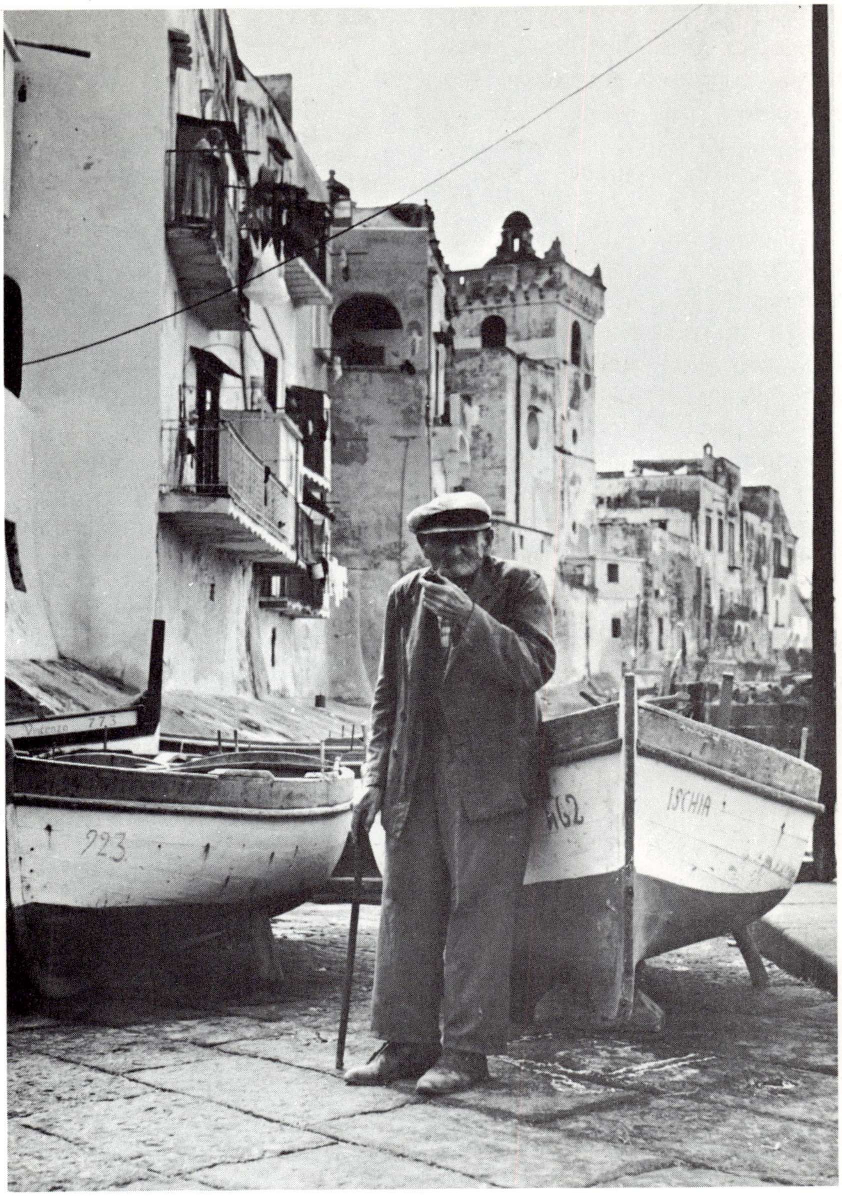
923
ISCHIA

SUGGESTED EXPOSURES FOR AVAILABLE-LIGHT PHOTOGRAPHY

Subjects	ASA 64	ASA 125	ASA 400	ASA 1000
Home interiors with bright light	1/15 sec at *f*/2	1/30 sec at *f*/2	1/30 sec at *f*/2.8-4	1/60 sec at *f*/4
Home interiors with average light	— — —	1/8 sec at *f*/2-2.8	1/30 sec at *f*/2	1/60 sec at *f*/2.8
Closeups by Candlelight	— — —	1/4 sec at *f*/2-2.8	1/15 sec at *f*/2	1/30 sec at *f*/2-2.8
Brightly lit City Streets	1/30 sec at *f*/2	1/30 sec at *f*/2.8	1/60 sec at *f*/2.8-4	1/125 sec at *f*/4
Christmas Lights	1 sec at *f*/4	1 sec at *f*/5.6	1/30 sec at *f*/2	1/30 sec at *f*/2.8-4
Neon Signs	1/30 sec at *f*/4	1/60 sec at *f*/4	1/125 sec at *f*/4-5.6	1/125 sec at *f*/8
Shop Windows	1/30 sec at *f*/2.8	1/30 sec at *f*/4	1/60 sec at *f*/4-5.6	1/60 sec at *f*/8
Skylines	4 sec at *f*/5.6	1 sec at *f*/2	1 sec at *f*/2.8-4	1 sec at *f*/5.6
Fireworks	1/30 sec at *f*/2.8	1/30 sec at *f*/4	1/60 sec at *f*/4-5.6	1/60 sec at *f*/8
Fireworks (time-motion studies)	5 sec at *f*/8	5 sec at *f*/11	5 sec at *f*/16-22	5 sec at *f*/32
Floodlit Buildings and Monuments	4 sec at *f*/5.6	1 sec at *f*/4	1/15 sec at *f*/2	1/30 sec at *f*/2-2.8
Night Football, Baseball, Racing	1/30 sec at *f*/2.8	1/60 sec at *f*/2.8	1/125 sec at *f*/2.8-4	1/250 sec at *f*/4

SUGGESTED EXPOSURES FOR DAYLIGHT PHOTOGRAPHY

Subjects	ASA 64	ASA 125	ASA 400	ASA 1000
Landscapes in bright sun	1/100-1/125 sec at f/11	1/125 sec at f/16	1/250 sec at "f/22	1/500 sec at f/22
Landscapes on overcast day	1/100-1/125 sec at f/5.6-8	1/125 sec at f/8-11	1/250 sec at f/11-16	1/250 sec at f/16-22
Portraits in sun Subject facing sun	1/100-1/125 sec at f/11	1/125 sec at f/16	1/250 sec at f/22	1/500 sec at f/22
Portraits in sun Subject backlit	1/100-1/125 sec at f/5.6-8	1/125 sec at f/8-11	1/250 sec at f/11-16	1/250 sec at f/16-22
Portraits on overcast day Subject facing position of sun	1/100-1/125 sec at f/5.6	1/125 sec at f/8	1/125 sec at f/11	1/125 sec at f16
Sports in sun Frame-filling, active figure	— — —	1/500 sec at f/8	1/500 sec at f/16	1/500 sec at f/22
Sports in sun General, team shot	1/250 sec at f/8	1/250 sec at f/11	1/250 sec at f/22	1/500 sec at f/22
Sunsets—Exposure for good sky color	1/250 sec at f/11	1/250 sec at f/16	1/500 sec at f/22	—
Beach, snow, or desert scenes in bright sun	1/100-1/125 sec at f/16	1/125 sec at f/22	1/500 sec at f/22	—
Street scenes with little shadow area	1/100-1/125 at f/11	1/125 sec at f/16	1/250 sec at f/22	1/500 sec at f/22
Street scenes with shadows Exposure for shadow detail	1/100-1/125 sec at f/5.6-8	1/125 sec at f/8-11	1/250 sec at f/11-16	1/500 sec at f/11-16

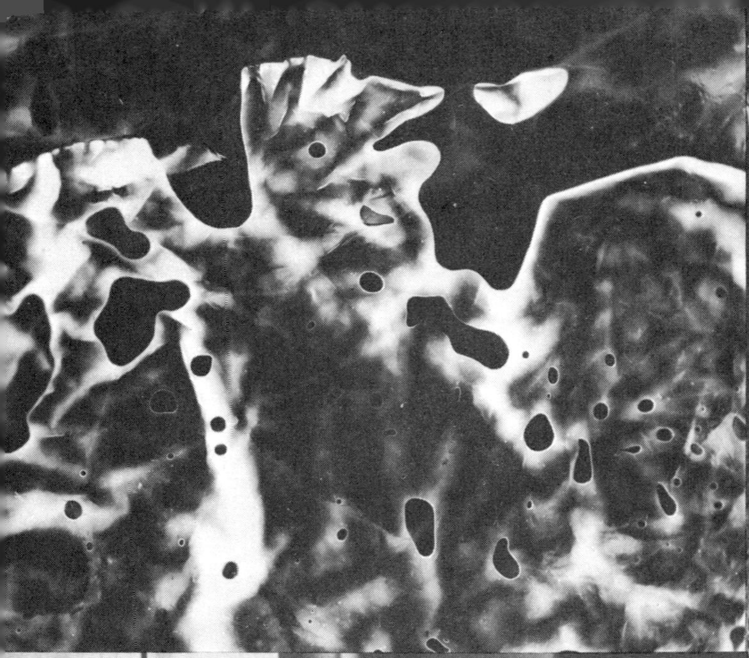

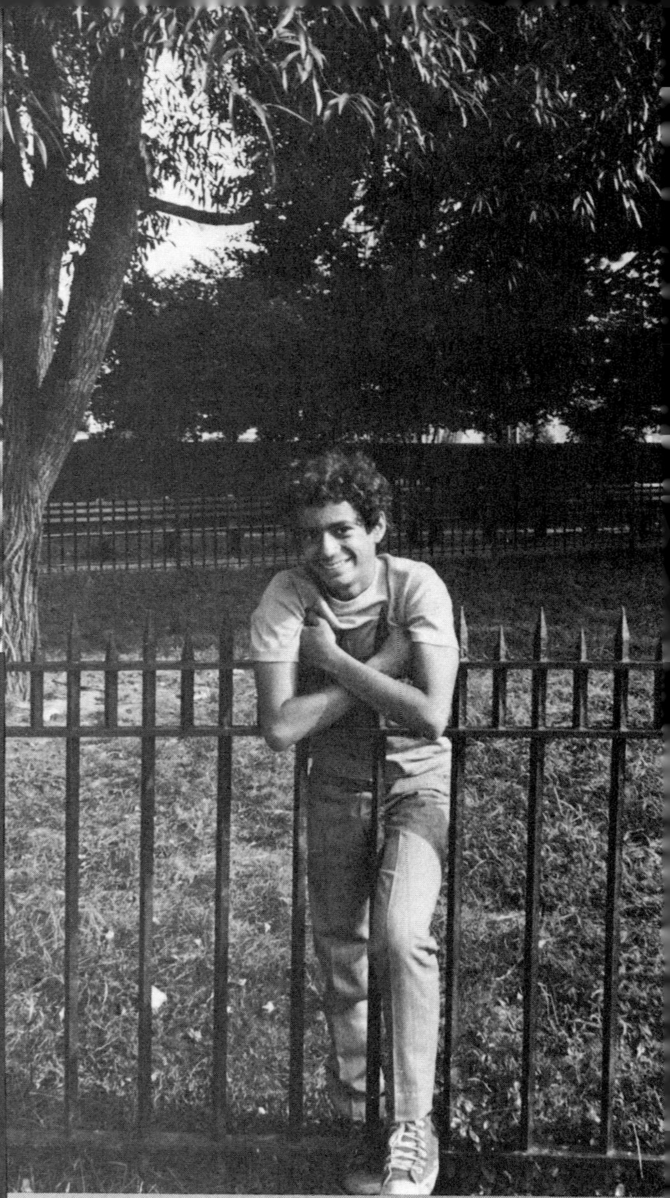

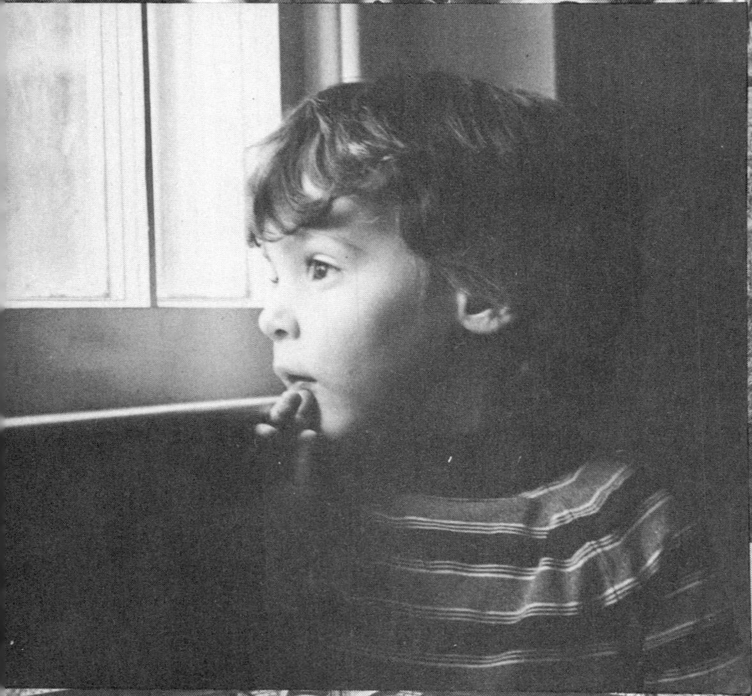

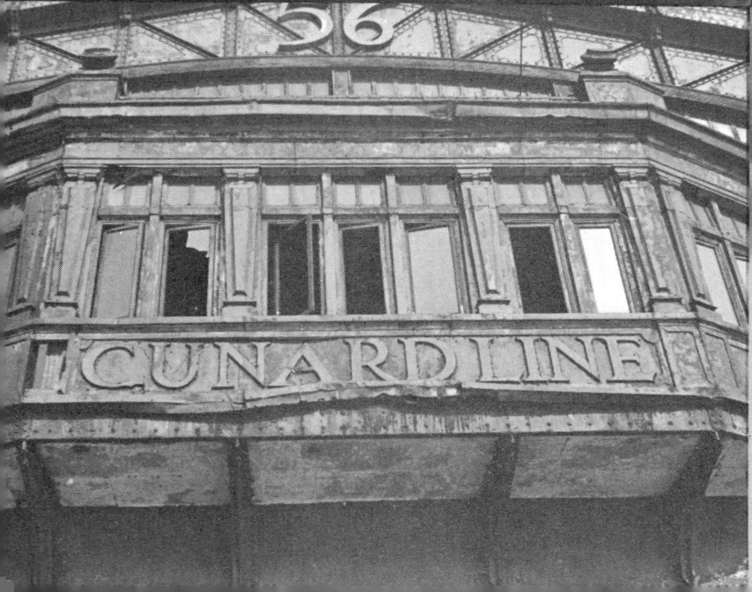
56
CUNARD LINE

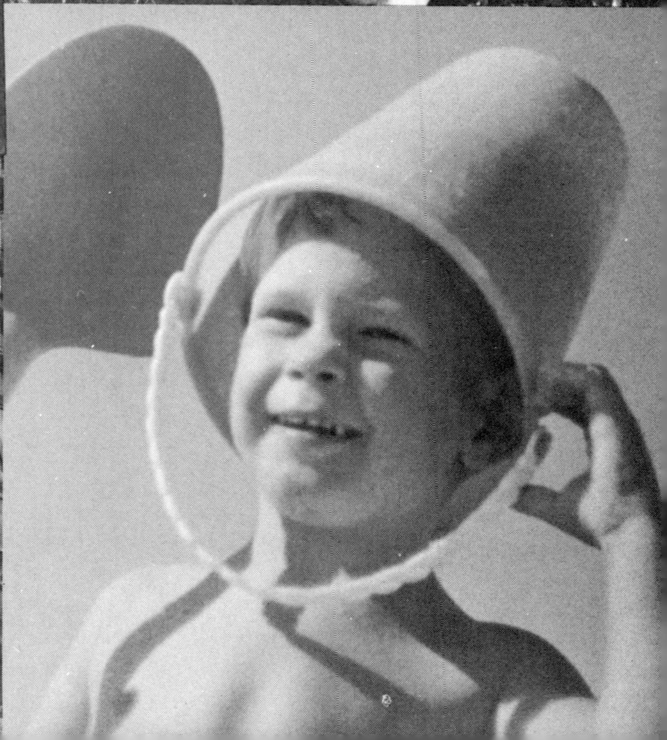